MERCEDES H
SL & SLC

ISBN 978-1-84155-704-5

CONTENTS

Mercedes Benz 350SLC   4

Mercedes Benz SL & SLC 1971-1989 Profile   8

Mercedes Benz 350SL 4.5   14

Mercedes Benz 380SL Specifications   18

Mercedes Benz 450SL Specifications   19

Mercedes Benz 560SL Specifications   20

Mercedes Benz SL and SLC Codes   21

Mercedes Benz 350SL Autotest   22

Mercedes Benz 350SL   27

Mercedes Benz 450SL Road Test   30

Mercedes Benz 380SLC Star Road Test   34

Mercedes Benz 450SLC Sports Coupe   40

R107 Buyers Guide   44

Mercedes Benz 560SL   51

Mercedes Benz 300SL Road Test   54

Mercedes Benz SL500 Silver Arrow   60

Mercedes Benz SL60 versus SL600   64

Mercedes Benz SL500   69

Mercedes Benz SL500 Road Test   74

Mercedes Benz SL65 Road Test   80

MERCEDES-BENZ 350SLC

Stuttgart's latest interpretation of the super-luxury coupe

JESSE ALEXANDER PHOTOS

WE WERE A bit surprised when the Mercedes-Benz 350SLC was introduced, as we hadn't expected the successor to the old big coupe, which was based on a sedan, to grow out of the sports model. Actually, it's a little misleading to say the SLC comes from the SL, as they were designed simultaneously and planned from the beginning as a pair. But the SL appeared first, so it's a natural to consider it an SL that's been stretched some 14 in. in the middle. The extra metal makes the wheelbase and overall length that much longer and provides room for a rear seat and a slightly larger trunk. The SLC has a fixed roof whereas the SL has a folding fabric one and a lift-off hardtop. Otherwise the two are very much the same car. All front-end sheet metal is interchangeable as are the doors, most exterior hardware and most of the front passenger compartment. The windshield is a smidgen taller on the SLC, as is the overall height. The SLC is 150 lbs heavier than the SL with both its roofs—a modest weight penalty for an extra 2- to 3-person carrying capacity and the added trunk space. If the SL seems heavy for its size, the SLC does not and it was probably the SL structure that was overdesigned to provide for the extra length of the SLC.

Whatever the technicalities, the SLC is a high-style prestige car. Whether or not the styling—probably somewhat compromised for the interchangeability—is successful is a matter the R&T staff couldn't even resolve among itself. Some consider the SLC better-looking than the SL, others say some serious compromises were made in proportions. All agreed that the slatted, fixed rear sections of the quarter windows look odd, and we concluded that they might be an afterthought solution to an awkward area of the car. Longer quarter windows would not roll down because of interference with the wheel wells, and yet Mercedes always designs good all-around vision into its cars. So the slats may have been adopted merely to avoid

the look of a 2-piece quarter window and still give the driver an extra few inches of vision.

Like any prestige car, the SLC is full of gadgets—most of which serve a useful purpose. As it should at $15,000 (that is approximate; the price is not firm at this time), it has a long list of standard equipment: air conditioning, automatic transmission, power steering and brakes (discs all around), stereo AM-FM radio with electric antenna, the best available radial tires, leather upholstery, electric window lifts, heated rear window and fog lights. Beyond that are the little gadgets: a central vacuum system that locks the right door, trunk and gas cap when the driver's door is locked; vacuum-restrained seatbacks that lock when the engine is running and the doors are closed (but have pushbutton overrides for rear passengers), a timer for the rear window heat, a removable map light in the glovebox, door panels that are heated or cooled by the heating or air conditioning, and a lighting position that operates either

the left-side or the right-side parking lights for parking on narrow, busy streets. The front seats have the usual Mercedes adjustable backrests, and in addition the track of the driver's seat can be raised or lowered.

As we mentioned in our test of the 350SL, ergonomics—which Funk & Wagnalls defines as "the study of the relationship between man and his working environment, with special reference to anatomical, physiological and psychological factors; human engineering"—were taken seriously in the layout of the interior and controls of these two models. The steering wheel is big, but by being so it clears the entire instrument cluster, which itself is extremely readable, and free from glare at night. And that wheel is the most fully padded one we've seen on any production car—itself a passive restraint device of the first order. Essential controls are near the steering wheel, are different from each other so there's no confusing them and, although they are so different from most other cars as to take some time for orientation, really clever and well thought out. There are two outside rearview mirrors, polarized and adjustable from the inside. Distribution of air from the climate control system is excellent, aided by those door ducts. And, for sheer entertainment value, the Becker Europa stereo radio in our test car was excellent in tone, separation and reception—it seems to have been improved from earlier versions we've tried.

The assembly quality is generally excellent, as you'd expect from Mercedes—a body that's solidly welded together, trim that fits, no rattles, nice (if not particularly lush) materials, good paint finish. All was not perfect, however, on this fairly early production example. The door handles and left seat adjuster were sticky, and the vacuum locking system wouldn't lock the right door. And though there was a total lack of any leaky wind noise around the windows when we began our test, some developed at the right front one 1000 miles or so later.

This test was longer than our usual one. We picked up the SLC in New Jersey, drove it into New York City for a day and then to Wilton, Conn., from where we began our long trek across the U.S. through the southeastern states, Texas, New Mexico and Arizona to our home base in coastal California. This 3500-mile journey subjected the SLC to a tremendous variety of conditions, as the reader can well imagine. New York was its usual summer self, 90-plus degrees and jammed. Here the SLC's air conditioning kept us cool and the engine never got over 230°F—cool as a cucumber, relatively speaking.

A hard rainstorm in New Jersey brought out two things: the first-rate behavior of the Michelin XVR tires and the excellent windshield wipers. Later in the trip, we used the wipers ⟫⟶

in rain at speeds up to 90 mph and found them still adequate. We do wish, however, that they would park farther down; they look pretty ugly to the driver, sticking up there above the instrument panel top when they're parked.

Later on, during the final leg across the desert toward San Diego, we found that the SLC's air conditioning, supposedly identical to that of the SL which we found wanting last year, was fully up to the job of keeping us cool in 110°, sunny weather. There were no rear-seat passengers for comment on conditions there, but at least the front seat was quite comfortable at an A/C setting just short of the full-tilt position that shuts off outside air.

A few more criticisms on interior matters. The sunvisors have a bent outboard edge that allows them to fit snugly against the ceiling when out of use, but this same bend prevents them from being positioned fully down against the windshield. We'd suggest a floppy edge like that in the Chevrolet Camaro to solve this slight annoyance. The electric windows are snail-like getting up and down. And the attachment of the shoulder belt to the lapbelt buckle is poorly designed: a slip of the elbow, or a push in the wrong place when securing the belt to its center fixture, will undo that shoulder belt.

In engine-transmission performance the 4.5-liter Mercedes models are a long way from the high-revving, jerky-shifting 6-cylinder Mercedes that acquainted the younger members of the R&T staff with the marque. This relatively large-displacement engine, used in the SLC, SL and 280-300 sedans, is a quiet, smooth unit that teams with an also smooth 3-speed torque-converter automatic transmission to give the sort of performance Americans expect in a luxury car. The combination isn't exactly quick, taking almost 11 seconds to get up to 60 mph, but it is effortless and about as responsive as we have any right to expect in these days of emission-controlled engines. And the electronic fuel injection keeps 1972-style drivability problems to a minimum. Things are rather leisurely getting off from a standing start but once the engine gets above 3000 rpm it begins to feel quite strong and even has a nice, subdued sound of power as it approaches its 5800-rpm limit. Fuel consumption is heavy: the 15.5-mpg figure is for everyday urban-suburban driving with the air conditioning off, and in highway cruising at 80-90 mph with the A/C on we got 12.5-13 mpg. The tank, supposed to take 23.8 gallons, took a maximum of 19.5 even after driving miles with the reserve light on, limiting cruising range to little more than 200 miles at high speed. The low fuel economy is a penalty we're all going to pay for emission control and low-octane fuel: the European version of this same engine, with a 9.0:1 cr and more advanced spark timing, would do 2 mpg better under the same conditions.

Mercedes' 3-speed automatic, new last year and used only with the 4.5 V-8 so far, is outstanding. Under most conditions its upshifts and downshifts are quite smooth, although a part-throttle upshift at low speeds can be a little rough. But its most laudable trait is its instant response to anything the driver wants from it. If he accelerates briskly in 2nd gear, then suddenly eases up, the gearbox doesn't hang about; it upshifts. If he selects a gear manually, he'd better be serious about it, for the gearbox shifts right then. And although drivers not used to it say it takes some acclimatization, the smoothly gated lever on the central console lends itself to manipulation without diversion of the driver's attention.

What about the chassis—ride, handling and braking? "Exemplary" describes all three. The SLC shares its chassis with the SL, of course, and this is Mercedes' most up-to-date engineering. The ride is about as good as it can be with steel springs and still be firm enough to give the kind of handling a Mercedes must have, and this holds true for any kind of road surface. As we've said of other Mercedes, the ride gets more impressive as the road gets worse. Drivers find they don't have to slow down for bumps and dips any more in a car like the SLC. We judged its ride somewhat better than the SL's.

The handling starts with M-B's ever-great power steering, quick (only three turns lock-to-lock) and, except for the low effort, as realistic in feel as the best rack-and-pinion manual steering. From there one can trace it through sophisticated suspension geometry that gives near-neutral response across the whole range and allows a slight, easily controllable oversteer to be induced by a burst of power or a quickly lifted throttle foot—a delight to the experienced driver but no threat to the inexperienced one. Finally, delivering all this to the ground were those great XVR tires on this test car—so good that they gave the SLC a quarter-g more cornering power than the lighter SL did on Dunlop SPs. One caution on these tires: for all their marvelous behavior one pays a price. They are wildly expensive to replace (well over $100 per tire) and they do not give long tread life.

Braking? Look at the figures. The stopping distances from 60 and 80 mph are both outstandingly short, and the average driver won't have any trouble keeping it under control while stopping like this though the rear wheels do want to lock up. We were surprised to get a little fade in our regular fade test, but it isn't enough to quibble about.

The newest member of our staff had a succinct way of summing up the 350SLC: he said that it is "the most complete car" he had ever driven. What he meant was that everything was done thoroughly. Everything hangs together; no loose ends anywhere. It's next to impossible to find fault with the car.

Controversy aside, nobody on the staff thought the SLC a beautiful car. That's subjective. But evaluating the engineering is an objective matter, and there's no question that it's the best. This car does its job well—from ambling around town to high-speed cruising to flailing about a winding mountain road to keeping its occupants comfortable and serene through it all. For $15,000 one expects a lot—and in the SLC one gets it. 🐂

COMPARISON DATA			
	Mercedes-Benz 350 SLC	Jensen Interceptor	Citroen SM
List price	$15,000	$14,500	$11,805
Curb weight, lb	3820	3905	3270
0-60 mph, sec	10.9	7.4	9.3
Standing ¼ mi, sec	18.4	16.0	17.4
Stopping distance from 80 mph, ft	253	300	300
Brake fade, 6 stops from 60 mph, %	12	25	nil
Cornering capability, g	0.725	0.750	0.722
Interior noise @ 70 mph, dBA	71	n.t.	n.t.
Fuel economy, mpg	15.5	12.0	15.9

Lift-up lid on package tray reveals first-aid kit.

ROAD TEST

MERCEDES-BENZ 350SLC

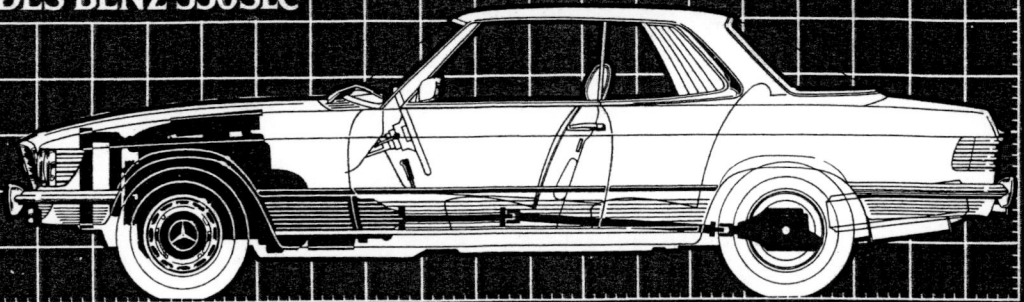

SCALE: 10" DIVISIONS

PRICE

List price, east coast....est $15,000
Price as tested,
   east coast ....est $15,000
Price as tested includes standard
equipment (air conditioning, automatic transmission, power
steering & brakes, stereo AM/FM
radio, fog lights, etc). dealer prep

IMPORTER

Mercedes-Benz of North America
158 Linwood Plaza, Fort Lee, N.J.

ENGINE

Type .... sohc V-8
Bore x stroke, mm ......92.0 x 85.0
  Equivalent in............3.62 x 3.35
Displacement, cc/cu in....4520/276
Compression ratio 8.0:1
Bhp @ rpm, net........195 @ 4500
  Equivalent mph.....................109
Torque @ rpm, lb-ft.....259 @ 3000
  Equivalent mph.....................72
Fuel injection........ Bosch electronic
Fuel requirement......regular, 91 oct
Emissions, gram/mile:
  Hydrocarbons.....................1.80
  Carbon Monoxide 18.8
  Nitrogen Oxides 2.04

CHASSIS & BODY

Layout ....front engine/rear drive
Body/frame .... unit steel
Brake system......... 10.9-in. vented
  disc front, 11.0-in solid disc
  rear; vacuum assisted
  Swept area, sq in 451
Wheels ....steel disc, 14 x 6½ J
Tires....... Michelin X 205/70VR-14
Steering type............. recirculating
  ball, power assisted
  Overall ratio 15.6:1
  Turns, lock-to-lock.............3.0
  Turning circle, ft.................37.9
Front suspension: unequal-length
  A-arms, coil springs, tube shocks,
  anti-roll bar
Rear suspension: semi-trailing arms,
  coil springs, tube shocks, anti-roll
  bar

INSTRUMENTATION

Instruments: 160-mph speedometer,
7000-rpm tach, 99,999 odometer,
999.9 trip odo, oil pressure, coolant temperature, fuel level, clock
Warning lights: brake-on, alternator,
fuel level, hazard, high beam, dir-
ectionals, seatbelts

DRIVE TRAIN

Transmission ..... automatic, torque
  converter with 3-sp planetary
  gearbox
Gear ratios: 3rd (1.00) 3.07:1
  2nd (1.46) 4.49:1
  1st (2.31) 7.10:1
  1st (2.31 x 2.50) 17.7:1
Final drive ratio.................. 3.07:1

CALCULATED DATA

Lb/bhp (test weight) 17.8
Mph/1000 rpm (3rd gear).....24.0
Engine revs/mi (60 mph)..... 2500
Piston travel, ft/mi............... 1400
R&T steering index 1.14
Brake swept area, sq in/ton......221

MAINTENANCE

Service intervals, mi:
  Oil change......................... 4500
  Filter change..................... 4500
  Chassis lube .... none
  Tuneup 9000
Warranty, mo/mi........... 12/12,000

GENERAL

Curb weight, lb 3820
Test weight 4085
Weight distribution (with driver),
  front/rear, % 55/45
Wheelbase, in 111.0
Track, front/rear 57.2/56.7
Length 186.6
Width 70.5
Height 52.4
Ground clearance.................... 5.4
Overhang, front/rear 32.7/42.9
Usable trunk space, cu ft........ 12.6
Fuel capacity, U.S. gal
  (see text) 23.8

ACCOMMODATION

Seating capacity, persons 4
Seat width, front/rear....2x21.5/49.0
Head room, front/rear......40.0/35.5
Seat back adjustment, degrees......60

RELIABILITY

From R&T Owner Surveys the average
number of trouble areas for all models surveyed is 11. As owners of
earlier model Mercedes-Benz reported 3 trouble areas, we expect
the reliability of the 350 SLC to be
much better than average.

ROAD TEST RESULTS

ACCELERATION

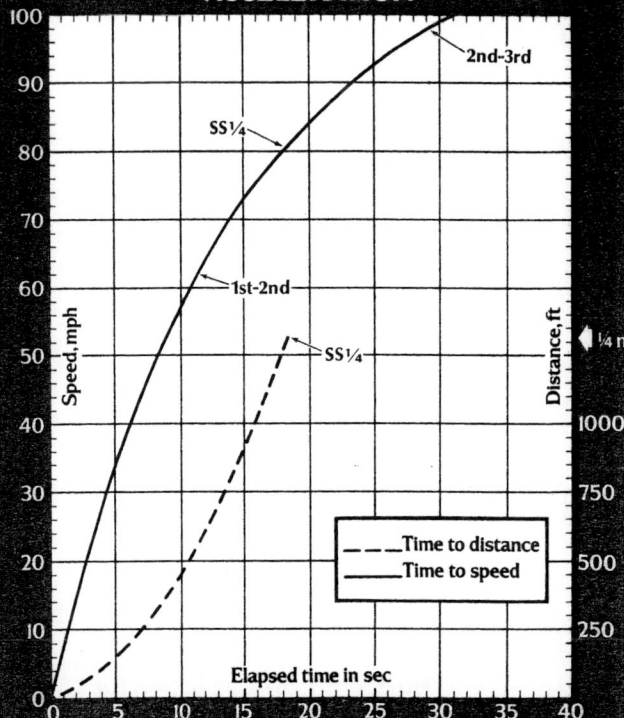

Time to distance, sec:
  0-100 ft................................4.0
  0-500 ....10.7
  0-1320 ft (¼ mi) 18.4
Speed at end of ¼-mi, mph....80.5
Time to speed, sec:
  0-30 mph 4.5
  0-40 mph 6.3
  0-50 mph 8.4
  0-60 mph 10.9
  0-70 mph 14.1
  0-80 mph 18.0
  0-100 mph 30.8

SPEEDS IN GEARS

3rd gear (5100 rpm) 124
2nd (5800) 98
1st (5800) 62

INTERIOR NOISE

All noise readings in dBA:
Idle in neutral 53
Maximum, 1st gear 75
Constant 30 mph 64
  50 mph 66
  70 mph 71
  90 mph 76

BRAKES

Minimum stopping distances, ft:
  From 60 mph 125
  From 80 mph 253
Control in panic stop...........good
Pedal effort for 0.5g stop, lb 17
Fade: percent increase in pedal ef-
  fort to maintain 0.5g deceleration
  in 6 stops from 60 mph 12
Parking: hold 30% grade? ....yes
Overall brake rating ...... very good

HANDLING

Speed on 100-ft radius, mph....33.0
Lateral acceleration, g 0.725

FUEL ECONOMY

Normal driving, mpg................15.5
Cruising range, mi.............see text

SPEEDOMETER ERROR

30 mph indicated is actually...27.0
50 mph 47.0
60 mph 57.0
70 mph 68.0
80 mph 78.0
Odometer, 10.0 mi 10.3

ACCELERATION

PROFILE

MERCEDES BENZ

SL & SLC
(1971~1989)

The evergreen W107 Mercedes SL/SLC remained in production from 1971 until last year. Is it a good classic buy? Martin Buckley finds out.
Photos by Julian Mackie and Tony Baker

FOR *Superb build quality, fantastic engineering, versatility, performance of 500SL, refinement, timeless style*

AGAINST *Not a sportscar, thirsty, basic-looking trim on early cars, not exclusive, six-cylinder cars lack performance*

The Mercedes SL is one of the Western World's most potent status symbols, classed with the heated swimming pool and the Rolex Oyster in the snob appeal stakes. It's not a question of exclusivity – after all, they proliferate in any of the West's wealthy cities. And it's not even as if the design is modern, or 'ultra hip': the first of the W107 SLs hit the streets in 1971 and the design changed hardly at all until its all-new replacement in 1989.

Now to you that might say a lot about the quality of the original engineering but it says more to me about Mercedes' ability to create a machine which carries an aura of timelessness, a slice of automotive glamour that has yet to go out of fashion after 18 years of production.

In many respects the SL's appeal is unique. Hard-top in place and you have the ultimate in two seater performance saloons, so civilised and draught free that it's difficult to believe the roof comes off at all. Top off, and the SL is transformed into a slick looking, sporting roadster – just the job if you want to show off your Mediterranean tan and tasteless gold jewellery. (Readers may detect a note of sarcasm in that last line but it has to be said that one

Left: Late 450 SLC, 14 inches longer than SL, has pillarless fix-head roof and room for four adults. Right: Design of chunky SL roadster is timeless though hardly subtle with heavy chrome detailing

of the most unfortunate aspects of SL ownership is the 'beautiful people' tag that goes along with it.

An SL is no sportscar either, so you can forget that idea if you are looking for a modern classic with a real sporting soul – the SL is just too comfortable. No, it's best to look on your old SL as a long-term possession – a beautifully engineered modern classic that could make a lot of sense.

When the W107 SL replaced the 'Pagoda' W113 car in 1971 it had a hard act to follow; it looked such a brute by comparison. Where the 230/250/280 Series cars had been pretty, almost delicate-looking, the W107 seemed bloated, nose-heavy and rather wedge-like. Squatting on its ultra-wide track and short wheelbase it was designed to appear heavy, as though it had been carved out of a solid billet of steel, tank-like and impregnable. The W107 succeeded because it was instantly recognisable as a Mercedes, a bullishly confident design.

The SLC coupe, developed alongside the SL, was a more subtle affair. Better looking, a better handler and much thinner on the ground. It proved something of a joker in the Mercedes pack, an SL sports-based car to replace the saloon-based W111 coupes and convertibles. The SLC replacement, the SEC, was based on the big 'S' class saloons of course. A longer, more elegant car using the front end of the SL but with an extra 14in of wheelbase and a smooth pillarless top allowing room to seat four in comfort. Those slats behind the rear window gave clearance for the side windows to wind right down without clashing with the rear wheelarches.

The two cars developed in parallel. Early cars, with the 3½-litre V8 and thumpy four-speed with fluid flywheel, were heavy drinkers and acceleration not too stunning. High speed cruising was their forte, with an added bonus of one of the best all-independent chassis in the business, the longer-wheelbase SLC having particularly fine balance qualities without the snappy oversteer tendencies of the stumpy two-seater *in extremis*.

The 450s that came later were the best of the seventies cars, the big iron blocker giving stump-pulling low down torque (the 350 was a bit feeble low down) with the added attraction of a silky smooth, responsive, three-speed with torque converter. There were no penalties in smoothness or fuel consumption with the smaller unit – about 14mpg overall but a lot more if you insisted on using the kickdown regularly. A weak point on the 450 was the lack of a limited slip diff as part of the standard equipment, which meant that a really brick-footed owner could burn a lot of rubber when the weight was transferred off either rear wheel when pulling out of a junction.

It was in that kind of situation, and in the ultimate subtilties of chassis refinement, that faster XJs always pulled one over on the SL and SLC, and of course there was always that little question of price. Where an XJS would have cost you £9527, a 450SLC would have set you back £11,522. What those figures don't tell you are the differences in quality between the two cars. The Mercedes was quite possibly the best engineered and styled car in the world, with even door gaps, a glass-smooth impenetrably thick coat of paint, a reputation for clocking up incredible mileages without major problems, and re-sale values that were in another world. The Jag, on the other hand, probably wasn't as well made as the top Ford Granada of the day and you only have to see a 12-year-old XJS and SLC side by side to have the Stuttgart quality message

rammed very firmly home.

Seventies SLs and SLCs had a rather clinical interior approach, even if the quality and execution were beyond criticism. Acres of high quality injection mouldings – often in very unprepossessing colours – were deemed adequate by Stuttgart. Some cars even boasted 'MB tex' (Merc-speak for vinyl) seats, or a combination of cheap-looking checked cloth for the centre section and tex for the side bolsters. Leather was optional and SLC coupés often had very savoury velour coverings. Power, windows, tape decks, and so on didn't necessarily come as standard on certain models, as this then hiked the price up even further if you wanted to bring equipment levels up to luxury car standards.

The success of the W.107 continued throughout the seventies but as the eighties dawned change was in the air. A new range of more efficient, lighter all-aluminium engines emerged, the 380 and 500, to replace the long-running iron-block 350 and 450 engines. They were joined by a new four-speed automatic transmission – as used in the Porsche 928 – and the long-awaited anti-lock brake option. For the first time in Britain you could buy a 280SL or (in theory, though I have never seen one) the SLC with twin-cam engine, and, if you wanted it, a rather unpleasant manual gearbox, also available (again in theory) on the 350. However, a manual change W107 SL of any sort is a rare sight in Britain, though much more common on the Continent, I suspect. The 280s were pleasant, sweet-engined cars but underpowered and not especially sparing in fuel.

Interior trim improved markedly around this time, with fillets of shiny veneer replacing the chilling plastic and a lot more equipment came as standard.

Above: High-sided SL cockpit has typically big wheel, logical dials. Below: Wood and leather interior of four-seater SLC with velour trim. Note pillarless side windows

Many regard the SLC as the nicest of th seventies Mercs, but it came to the end of the road i 1981 with the introduction of the S-class based SEC The 5.0-litre 450 SLC, with its lightweight panels and lhd 500 SLC were never considered.

But on the SL sauntered regardless; a replace ment always rumoured to be just round the corne yet selling strong right to the end of its days. Ther were a couple of new engines in '85 – the 420 an 6-cylinder 300 – and the American market even sa the 5.6-litre unit which transformed the urban Country Club cruiser into a bit of a hot rod. *Road an Track* dubbed it 'the German Corvette'. In a tigl spot the 560 (and to a certain extent the Europea 500) could really kick its tail out in a very un-Mer like fashion.

In September last year the W107 finally died, i heir what is perhaps the first truly exciting, tru sporting Mercedes SL since the original 300. Th waiting list for the new car is endless, but I can't he thinking that if Mercedes wanted to keep on makir the W107, the buyers would keep on lapping it up.

CONTEMPORARY ROAD TESTS

Motor, December 1971 (350 SL)
"A two-seater saloon sounds like a contradiction terms but as a generic title it fits the Mercedes 3 SL admirably. It's rather too big and heavy to quali as a sportscar even though its superb handling a roadholding – especially impressive in the wet – a more than a match for many that do. "
Car and Driver, October 1971 (350 SL)
"Even with the V8, performance of the new SL

PRODUCTION HISTORY

April 1971: 350 SL W107 launched with type M116 iron block, 3499cc, ohd V8, four-speed manual or four-speed auto, optional hard top, power steering standard, LSD optional. British imports begin June 1971.

July 1971: W107 launched on North American market as 350 SL 4.5 with bigger, detoxed M117 4520cc unit. US market model has twin round lights, large rubber overriders. Auto only.

February 1972: 350 SLC introduced after launch at the Paris Show, October 1971. Wheelbase longer by 14.1 inches. Front end bodywork identical but with four seats and different pillarless fixed roof. Mechanically identical.

March 1973: 450 SL/SLC introduced in Europe. 350 4.5 US models now also known as 450s, and 350s continue.

September 1974: 280 SL and SLC introduced with 185bhp M110 twin-cam in-line six, lower 3.69 final drive and 185 section tyres. Four/five-speed manual or new four-speed auto with torque converter. No UK imports until October 1980.

October 1977: 450 SLC 5.0-litre announced at the Frankfurt Show, with production cars available the following Spring. Visually distinguished by dark-coloured lower body panels, chin spoiler and small boot spoiler, the 5.0 used a new light alloy 5025cc version of the 4½-litre M117, alloy bonnet and boot lid and wheels. Auto only.

February 1980: 350 and 450 SLCs replaced by 380 and 500 models with light alloy 4973cc and 3818cc V8s and four-speed automatic. LSD and hardtop now standard, ABS an option, alloy bonnet and boot lid. UK sales begin October 1980.

September 1981: SLC coupes discontinued and 280/380 and 500 SL models get 'energy concept revisions' (higher axle ratio, revised valve timing).

November 1985: 280 and 380 SLs replaced by 300 and 420 models. 300 has new M103 sohc in-line six, the 420 a 4196cc version of 380 unit with modified combustion chambers etc. Visual changes include chin spoiler, new design of alloy wheels.

August 1989: W107 Production ends.

PRODUCTION FIGURES

350 SL	15,304
350 SLC	13,925
350 SL 4.5/450 SL	66,298
350 SLC (US) 450 SLC	65,715
280 SL	15,676
280 SLC	10,666
450 SLC 5.0/500 SLC	2796
380 SL	22,743
380 SLC	3789
300 SL	13,742
420 SL	2148
500 SL	11,812

much the same as the old one. Passing ability is slightly better with the 350 but it is decidedly more sluggish in low speed situations... Nor are we excited by the SL's handling. The low-pivot swing axle of the 280 SL has given way to that of the 'new generation' sedans. This makes the 350 more predictable at its limits but it's still ragged – understeering strongly, but occasionally breaking loose at the rear to swing its tail wide."
Road and Track, November 1972 (350 SLC)
"Things are rather leisurely getting off from a standing start but once the engine gets above 3000rpm it begins to feel quite strong and even has a nice, subdued sound of power as it approaches its 5800rpm limit... Upshifts and down shifts are quite smooth although a part-throttle upshift at low speeds can be a little rough... The ride is about as good as it can be with steel springs and yet still remain firm

enough to give the kind of handling a Mercedes must have. Our newest member of staff had a succinct way of summing up the 350 SLC: he said that it is 'the most complete car' he had ever driven... 'everything hangs together: no loose ends anywhere. It's next to impossible to find a fault with the car'."
Car and Driver, January 1977 (450 SL)
"... In spite of its 'sports' appellation, the 450 SL is more Mercedes than sportscar, more an unbreakable piece of sober engineering than a berserk street burner. When a really experienced driver, who understands the chassis and the engine manners of the car, who knows how to squeeze every last bit of performance from the three-speed automatic transmission, and who is less interested in caressing his status symbol than flat getting it down some bit of twisty madness, steps in. In hands like his the 450 SL becomes a car with very high limits, in spite of its bulk, in spite of its detuned power train and in spite of its trendy value to the country club set."
Car and Driver, February 1980 (L.J.K. Setright on the 450 SLC 5.0-litre)
"This is the car in which, in blissful legality on the public highway, and in perfect and tactful safety among all manner of other people going about their daily drives, I averaged 133mph over 20 miles, 126mph over 40 miles. This is a car that is every bit as fast as it looks and which displays its incomparable pedigree by being very much faster than it feels."

DRIVING IMPRESSIONS

As we have said, a W107 SL is no sportscar in the accepted sense. It is more a restful, satisfying and untemeramental mile-eater, soft-edged, easy-going and efficient in everything it does.

The first thing that hits you is the absolute solidity of the body: massive, hefty doors that shut with a deeply reassuring thunk, plastic trim that doesn't creak and shudder and vast, unyielding seats. Back in the seventies when our S-registered 350 SL was built, D-B made no attempt to soften the visual blow of that wasteland of injection-moulded plastic on the dash with token-gesture slabs of wood, and the seat covering has the bare-faced cheek to look exactly

what it is – plastic. Only Mercedes could get away with that. A massive ship's tiller of a steering wheel and a legible set of instruments complete the cabin picture.

The V8 engine gives an impression of fussyness when extended, but it actually revs far more willingly then many big V8s, belting out its torque most enthusiastically in the 3500-4500rpm range, when the unit takes an aggressive snarl. There isn't an abundance of low speed torque so the acceleration with the three-speed auto box in tow doesn't thrill. As the throttle is depressed, the tail squats, sending the nose rearing up into the air, but fat tyres make wheel-spin a wet-roads-only indulgence, and every one of those 200 horses had to be sent to the rear wheels to get even a hint of tail wag. Conversely, easing off mid-corner in the wet (even at quite sedate speeds) could make the tail move a good foot or so out of line.

The steering is direct and sensitive, if not pin sharp- there's a degree of straight-ahead numbness and a touch too much assistance. Very little cornering lean is generated and the general attitude is on the mild, understeer, side of neutrality. The three-speed gearbox gets top marks for its changes, each gear flowing almost seamlessly into the next with only a slur in engine note to tell you it's changed. Kick down is quite violent if you use the last few millimetres of throttle travel.

TECHNICAL DESCRIPTION

On its introduction in 1971, the European market 350 SL used the type M116 V8 engine, first seen in the 280 SE 3.5 in 1969. A 90° unit, with an iron cylinder block and an alloy head, it displaced 3499cc (92 × 65.8mm) and had a sohc for each bank, chain-driven, with finger-type followers operating in-line valves. The four-throw crankshaft ran in five sturdy main bearings. Lubrication was by a gear-type pump, drive by a roller chain off the crankshaft. The fuel system was by Bosch electronic injection with automatic cold start enrichment. Running a 9.5:1 compression ratio, maximum power was 200bhp at 5800rpm, with a peak torque figure of 211lb/ft at a high

Above: The SL two-seater roadster combined sportscar features and performance. Left: Refined 500 SL roadster boasts perfect fitting soft-top. Right: Snug John Bolster road-testing SL with Pagoda hard-top in place

11

4.5-litre V8 unit offered electronic fuel injection and sohc, developing 225bhp

1. The W107 project was known as 'der Panzer-wagen' during its development because the engineers reckoned it was built like a tank.

2. The SLC coupe, which came out after the SL in February 1972, was actually developed alongside the two-seater as a replacement for the W111 two-door models, though no convertible version was ever envisaged.

3. From the beginning, North American market SLs came with the 4½-litre V8 engine and were initially entitled the 350 SL 4.5. The European market cars received bigger engine in 1973.

4. Slats incorporated behind SLC coupe's rear windows, giving glass room to wind down all the way for a full pillarless effect.

5. American market SLs and SLCs suffered greatly at the hands of emission controls: by 1980 a federal 450 SL was putting out 160bhp and was only good for 112mph and 0-60 in 11 seconds with 16mpg fuel consumption.

6. Teldix-ATE anti-lock brakes were listed as an option when the SL was introduced in 1971, but an ABS facility was not actually available until 1980.

7. The W107 SL didn't need a roll bar in the manner of the Triumph Stag because its computer-designed screen pillars proved 50 per cent stiffer than on the previous model.

8. From the mid-eighties onwards there was a 560 SL, but only for the American market. Its performance was similar to the European 500 SL.

9. Though bigger, and rather heavier, the SLC coupes were considered to have sweeter, less twitchy handling than the shorter wheelbase SLs.

10. Perhaps the most sought after of the W107s is the 450 SLC 5.0, a limited production performance model with lightweight panels, spoilers front and rear and a 240bhp light alloy 5025cc V8. Production ended in 1981 with less than 3000 built.

4000rpm, and 6500rpm rev limit.

Modified to comply with 1972 American emission requirements, the M116 unit was woefully underpowered – a lower compression ratio, retarded spark advance, and leaner fuel mixtures took their toll. So, from the beginning, the US market model was given the 4½-litre unit with a taller cylinder block, new crankshaft and a longer stroke up from 65.8 to 84.7mm, giving a total displacement of 4520mm. Bigger combustion chambers and a lower compression of 8:1 were other features, resulting in 195bhp at 4500rpm and a healthy 259lb/ft of torque at 5900rpm. When it eventually became available in Europe there was 225bhp at 5000rpm on tap, with 278lb/ft of torque at 3000rpm.

The engine used in the 450 SLC 5.0-litre was something of a one-off, though it retained the M117 designation, as it was closely based on this unit. Over-bored from 92 to 97mm to give a capacity of 5025cc, the cylinder block, heads, pistons valve covers, and sump were all cast in Reynolds 390 light alloy, saving some 95lb compared with the cast-iron unit. K-Jetronic mechanical injection was used, hydraulic tappets replaced the adjustable tappets and there were special head gaskets to eliminate the need for re-torquing the heads at the first service. Claimed output was 240bhp and 297lb/ft of torque.

The 380 and 500 engines replaced the 350 and 450 units in 1980, but the basic architecture was as before, though the capacity of the 5.0-litre had come down from 5025cc to 4973cc by way of narrower cylinder bores. Peak horsepower was still 240bhp.

American market 380 engines had a slightly larger 3839cc displacement to allow for some reshaping of the combustion chambers for emissions-related reasons. From May 1981 European 380 SLs had this displacement too, producing 204bhp at 5250rpm. The 280 SL used the M110 twin overhead camshaft 2746cc in-line six, with a seven main-bearing bottom end and Bosch electronic fuel injection for an output of 185bhp at 6000rpm and 175lb/ft of torque at 4500rpm. That was replaced in 1985 by the new M103 2962cc single overhead cam all-alloy in-line six with Bosch KE injection and a four main-bearing crankshaft. Advertised power for the 300 SL was 190bhp at 5600rpm with 192lb/ft of torque at 4250rpm. The V8 420 SL introduced at the same time to replace the 380 used yet another variation on the faithful M116 theme, stroked from 71 to 78mm and putting out 218bhp-14bhp up on the 380 with its larger inlet valves and improved injection.

The W107s have used a bewildering range of transmissions. The 350 SL/SLC could have a four-speed all-synchromesh box, again as featured in the 280 SE 3.5 saloon, or more commonly the D-B four-speed automatic with its antiquated fluid flywheel. Later 350's (and all American market 350 4.5s) used a new three-speed with torque converter unit. The 450 could not be bought with a manual gearbox. All 500s, 380s, 420s and 300s had a new four-speed automatic. 280 SL/SLCs had either the four-speed manual, a five-speed manual with overdrive top, the three-speed autobox or, later, a four-speeder.

At the front all models used double wishbone suspension with tubular shocks, coil springs, an anti-roll bar and anti-dive geometry. At the back, splayed trailing arm suspension was employed with the arms pivoted on a substantial cross member that also carried the final drive unit. There was coil springing and an anti-roll bar and the larger V8-engined versions had anti-squat geometry. Assisted recirculating ball steering was a universal W107 fitment, and wheels were either pressed steel with hub caps or forged light alloy castings. Braking was naturally by discs all round, internally vented at the front and solid at the back with separate rear drums and split front and rear circuits. An anti-lock system became an option from 1980 onwards.

The body of the SL and SLC is of unitary construction with all-steel outer body panels and front and rear crumple zones. The two-seater SL had an optional steel hardtop with vents for the extraction of stale air with the hood neatly hidden under a metal cover. The SLC coupe was 14.1 inches longer in its wheel base, 1.8 inches taller and was a full four-seater.

BUYER'S SPOT CHECK

One of the best reasons for buying a Mercedes SL has to be for its strength and reliability. But to get some idea of the kind of things that *can* go wrong we talked to Mercedes specialist Robert Schmitt, of Kilburn, in North London.

Engine and transmission: Schmitt: "A lot of our customers obviously drive in town a great deal causing a build-up of dirt and petrol in the oil which thins it out. This causes the camshaft ❶ to start tapping and the engine then begins to use oil. Early 350s and 450s were knocking out camshafts all the time – especially the right-hand bank, but then they modified the oil pipe that goes across the top to give a better feed to the rear bearing. The secret is to change the oil as regularly as is practicable. I always recommend synthetic oil. Oil leaks sometimes out of the front seal, but most come from the rocker box cover.

"In 1976 they changed the fuel injection on the V8s from electronic to mechanical. It's pretty reliable, but problems can arise with the distributor and injectors if water gets into the system. On the early V8s there was quite a lot of trouble with under bonnet fires when petrol hoses and injectors leaked under cold-start pressure, but most of these have now been modified. Petrol pumps fail occasionally and warm-up regulators go quite often on the later cars – when cold they won't rev and start popping and banging.

We do quite a lot of timing chain work on V8s – if they rattle for the first few seconds after they start up you know they need changing but usually, a top-end job, doing the valve guides and seals and so on, will cure any oil burning. Ideally, what you are looking for is 45kg/cm squared oil pressure at tickover cold, or at speed with everything warm.

"The twin cam is a nice engine, but it can fly apart through lack of oil. Again, like the V8s, you get a lot of petrol in the oil around town. So when you blat down the motorway, the engine gets hot, burns off the petrol and then all of a sudden there's no oil. The twin cam is more likely than a V8 to throw a rod out of the side".

"On really early twin cams the drive gears that drive the oil pump used to break up, so you had no oil feed, which meant the cam boxes would lock up – a major operation to put right. Early ones used to have a slight vibration but they put a counter weight on the crankshaft front web."

"So many owners want to mess about with these cars themselves, and then come to us to put it right. On the later cars, everything is electric: electric solenoids everywhere, which luckily means people don't tend to interfere with them. On the older cars people play around more because there aren't things like electric idles and they probably can't afford to have them done by a specialist. They usually end up here, or in a place like this, anyway.

"The early four-speed gearbox with its fluid flywheel had problems, the brake band would slip and judder when you pulled away, but there are no real snags with the other boxes. Just look for harsh changes which could mean wear in the friction bands or the hydraulic valves."

Bodywork: "You don't see many rusty SLs but it can happen. It all depends on how they have been treated. A common place is round where the hardtop fits on the rear scuttle, because water has a habit of sitting rather than running away and eventually rust can start eating into the steel lid that covers the soft-top. They can rust to a certain extent on the front wings around the arches ❷ and headlamps, and on really old ones the sills can hole. The rear box sections ❸ on the chassis might even need welding up.

The windscreen ❹ can come unbonded and start letting water into the interior. Boot leaks are also quite common and you may find that the rear lamps have let water in. The rubber seals around the doors get flattened after a number of years which means a lot of wind noise. The headlamp adjusters commonly seize up and the headlamp bowls themselves often seize up. The front cross-member that holds the bumper can rot after a few years.

On the SLC the side electric windows often seize up and on the late ones the regulators do the same. The slats behind the rear window tend to discolour."

Suspension Steering and brakes: "Brakes are pretty trouble-free but like any heavy, automatic car they go through pads and front discs ❺ very quickly. Steering boxes ❻ can get a bit of play in them after a few miles but if you have them adjusted by half a turn every time the car goes in for a service, the problem never arises.

I've never had to change a ball joint on one, although shock absorbers do tend to leak when they get old. Engine mountings give up eventually, as does the centre prop bearing."

COMPETITION HISTORY

The big SLC Coupé might seem like an unlikely competition car but in the late seventies a number of factory-prepared cars were campaigned successfully by private entrants in long-distance rally events.

The 450 SLC's first outing was in 1978 on the South American Rally or the *Vuelta a la America Sud* as it was officially titled. Four cars were entered in a relatively standard form with untuned engines and automatic transmissions. The British pairing of Colin Malkin and Andrew Cowan won the event outright,

Perplexed and unimpressed audience watch SLC's antics on East Africa Rally, 1980

with Sobieslaw Zasada's SLC coming in second. Though handicapped by a roll Timo Makinen came in fourth and set all the fastest stage times. The event itself was gruelling, passing through all ten countries of the South American continent (18,500 miles).

A 450 SLC 5.0-litre driven by Hannu Mikkola came second in the East Africa Safari in 1979, and in the same year on the Bandama Rally on the Ivory Coast of West Africa, SLCs took the first four places, driven by Mikkola, Waldegard, Andrew Cowan and Vic (junior) Preston. Unfortunately the 500 SLCs fielded during 1980 suffered mechanical problems and failed to notch up a single win.

An AMG modified 450SLC had a brief spell of glory, entered for group 2 racing in 1979, and succeeded in finishing a creditable third in its first outing at Monza. Hampered by weight and an auto box, it couldn't out-pace the BMW CLs.

PRICES

No bargains here. Even an early, tired 350 SL or SLC can still realise the best part of £7000, and £12,000 would be nearer the mark for a nice car. Robert Schmitt had a 1976 350 on his books that he has sold three times over the last three years and the price hadn't fluctuated by more than £500 during that period… The basic 280 SL ranges between £22,000 for a top-notch '85 car to around £9500 for a lesser, higher-mileage 1980 model. The last of the 450s could still fetch £14-£15,000, which is around the bottom line for a 500 SL: the last of the 500s are now selling for a considerable premium – £45,000 or so, because the waiting list for the new car is so long. SLC coupes come slightly cheaper but really nice, late cars are now reaching £20,000.

SPECIFICATION	MERCEDES-BENZ 280 SL	MERCEDES-BENZ 450 SLC
Engine	In-line six	V8
Bore/stroke	86mm × 78.8mm	92mm × 85mm
Capacity	2746cc	4520cc
Valves	Dohc	Sohc per bank
Compression ratios	9:1	8.8:1
Power	185bhp (DIN) at 6000rpm	225bhp (DIN) at 5500rpm
Max Torque	170lb/ft at 4500rpm	278lb/ft at 3000rpm
Fuel system	Bosch D-Jetronic injection	Bosch D-Jetronic injection
Transmission	Four/five-speed manual or four-speed auto	Three-speed auto
Brakes	Discs all round	Discs all round
Front suspension	Ind by twin wishbones, coil springs, anti-roll bar	Ind by twin wishbones, coil springs, anti-roll bar
Rear suspension	Ind by semi-trailing arms, coil springs, anti-roll bar	Ind by semi-trailing arms, coil springs, anti-roll bar
Steering	Recirculating ball, power-assisted	Recirculating ball, power-assisted
Body/Chassis	Integral steel body	Integral steel body

DIMENSIONS		
Length	14ft 4.1in	15ft 7in
Width	5ft 10in	5ft 10in
Wheelbase	8ft 0.9in	9ft 3in
Weight	3307lbs	3795lbs

PERFORMANCE		
Max speed	127mph	134mph
0-60mph	9.5sec	8.5sec
Typical mpg	20mpg	14mpg

PERFORMANCE COMPARISON	Mercedes Benz 350 SL	BMW 3.0CS	Jensen Interceptor
Max speed	126mph	131mph	137mph
0-60mph	9.3sec	8.0sec	6.4sec
Standing ¼ mile	17sec	16.2sec	15sec
Overall mpg	14mpg	20mpg	12mpg

Technical Analysis

MERCEDES-BENZ 350SL 4.5

The sporting Mercedes is more than a match for U.S. regulations—but it's a close match

A LARGER, HEAVIER car using an engine with increased displacement and reduced efficiency surely tops the list of cars Mercedes-Benz doesn't want to build and wouldn't build if there was any choice. Which there isn't, our very own government having decreed that cars get heavier in the interests of safety and weaker in the interests of reduced emissions.

There Mercedes was, in a sense, with the 280SL in one hand and a set of future crash and emissions standards in the other. The 280SL was selling well and meeting the current rules without hardship but the body would need reinforcement in front, back and sides for bumper and side penetration regulations coming soon, and the engine would require power-reducing changes to conform to the 1972 pollution levels. It could have been done but the result would have been a new car that looked old, didn't perform on the level expected of a luxury grand tourer and still lacked some engineering improvements already in use on the smaller Mercedes sedans. Ergo, a new car, to allow changes and improvements in the best possible manner with fewer compromises and a sales appeal not possible beneath 8-year-old body panels.

Engine and Transmission

IN EUROPE the new car is simply the 350SL, designating a sports car with the 3.5-liter V-8 announced earlier for midrange Mercedes sedans. For the U.S., Mercedes retreats once again from the admirable system of naming cars for engine size. The proper name for the car we'll get is 350SL 4.5, the last digits telling us that the engine displaces 4.5

liters. Why and how this comes about is a bit sad.

Six-plus years and uncounted millions of dollars worth of research have not greatly benefited the piston engine. The engineers in Stuttgart, Detroit, Milan, etc., have learned a great deal about combustion and its products and byproducts. They have not managed to increase power while persuading blossoms to spew out the exhaust. Rather the reverse: changes that reduce hydrocarbons, carbon monoxide and oxides of nitrogen also reduce power. For adequate power within the specified controls, alas, bigger is better; apparently big power from small displacement isn't compatible with low emissions at ordinary speeds.

Mercedes started with the 3.5 V-8 introduced last year for the 280SEL. In its 1970-certified form the 3.5 performed well, albeit we noted that the emission controls caused it to feel strained under some conditions.

That was only the beginning. Because of the timing of the 350SL's introduction, Mercedes wished to have the car qualify for sale under the 1972 rules. What was required, in general, was a retarded spark advance and fuel mixtures leaned almost to the critical point. And the compression ratio had to be reduced, mostly to lower the oxides of nitrogen (NO_x).

Thus modified, the 3.5 engine had no power left. So Mercedes retained the basic engine, with sohc, Bosch fuel injection, transistor ignition et al. The 92-mm bore applies to both 3.5 and 4.5 engines. But the U.S. version has a taller cylinder block, new crankshaft and longer stroke, up from 65.8 mm to 84.7 mm. This adds one full liter of displacement. The 4.5 cylinder heads have enlarged combustion chambers, for

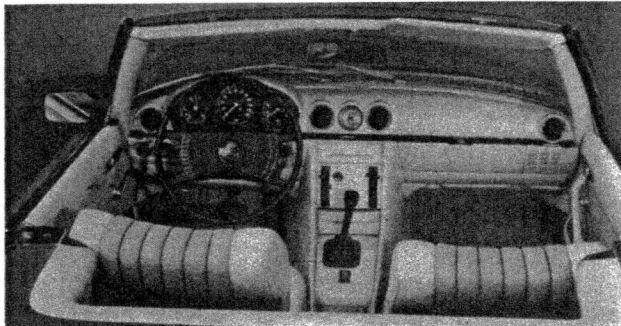

MERCEDES·BENZ 350SL 4.5

a low compression ratio of 8:1. The fuel and ignition changes needed for hydrocarbon and carbon monoxide control raised combustion temperatures and NO_x and the lower c.r. is needed to drop temperatures and NO_x to within the law. Ouch. As another dubious benefit, the 4.5 can be operated on unleaded fuel. Sure, Mercedes knows this is a political issue, just as Detroit knows it. But it's an issue impossible to fight, so Mercedes had to go along.

Anyway, the bigger engine with lower compression ratio is within the 1972 regulations and can meet the standards until 1974. Seeing that nobody knows if the 1975 standards can be met, Mercedes is readier than anybody else.

After all that, we break even. The 3.5 V-8 produces 230 bhp by SAE rating method and 200 bhp by DIN measurement. The U.S. 4.5 does exactly the same at lower engine speed. We know therefore, that it takes another full liter of displacement to make up for emissions-based spark curves and fuel mixtures and a drop of 1.5 points of c.r.

The immediate penalty is surprisingly small. The cost of making different blocks and cranks isn't too high and the planning for them was already taken care of since the possibility of enlarging the engine was taken into account when the V-8 was designed. And the engineers said that they would have been put to the expense of running myriad certification tests for either the 3.5 or the 4.5.

The cost comes later, when the car is being operated. The 4.5 requires 10% more fuel than the 3.5 to do a given amount of work. The fuel isn't being used as efficiently, so more fuel is needed. It's as simple, and as depressing, as that.

The 4.5 brings with it an entirely new transmission. It's an automatic and something of a departure for Mercedes, having a torque converter with three forward speeds while other M-B automatics use a fluid coupling and four speeds. The torque converter multiplies torque, which the 4.5 has in good supply anyway, so three speeds are adequate. None were available for test at the time of the 350SL's European introduction and the intermediate ratios hadn't been decided, so there are no details out yet.

The automatic will be the only transmission offered in the 350SL 4.5. Emissions laws again. Because of the variation in engine speeds and loads, the engine would need a second set of spark and fuel calibrations and a second set of certification tests. The 280SL came with 4-speed manual or automatic, and 30% of the buyers opted for the 4-speed. Mercedes had to go with the majority.

Body and Styling

As a replacement, the 350SL has the same basic configuration as the 280SL: a 2-passenger convertible with a choice of soft top, hard top or both. Trunk space is commensurate with passenger capacity and the area behind the seats can be fitted with (optional) shaped padding for two children.

Shopworn though it is, the most accurate description of the new body is that old favorite—longer, lower, wider. The specifications are printed elsewhere in this article, so to avoid repetition we'll sum up by saying that the change from 280SL to 350SL brings increases of 2.4 in. of wheelbase, 3.3 of overall length and 0.5 of width, and a reduction of 0.2 in. of height.

To understand, you need a rulebook. In 1973, cars sold in the U.S. must withstand collisions of 5 mph front and 2.5 mph rear without damage to lights, fuel tank or other safety-related systems. The most practical way to meet the rules is simply to use more metal, more in both the sense of dimension and of strength. Especially when the threat of battering-ram bumpers looms. Heavier bumpers (they will add an estimated 120 lb) need heavier brackets, etc. Mercedes still believes in controlled crushability, that former safety feature since converted into an insurance liability, and the 350SL retains fore and aft sections that collapse before the people-space contorts. But it took more metal in all three areas.

Mercedes engineering did some good work here. It's a unit body, as all Mercedes have been for as long as we can remember, with a shaped floor pan and the cowling, rear structure, door posts, etc., are welded to that. All steel, while the 280SL used some aluminum panels. The new pan allowed the fuel tank to be moved from beneath the trunk to between the rear wheels, out of harm's way.

The doors and their mounts were designed to resist side force in the manner pioneered by General Motors but using the shape and size of the doors, rather than GM's separate barriers fastened to the doors inside the body panels.

The most intricate planning involves the windshield pillars. Mercedes provides rollover protection with (another area of possible future legislation) pillars that are very strong, yet thin. M-B bills this as a breakthrough in stress analysis. Calculating the strength of a 2-dimensional component is easy. But the total mathematics required to analyze the strength of an intricate part when attacked from a nearly-infinite number of angles would take years of human effort. Mercedes instead tots up all the possible stresses and feeds them to a computer. Minutes later the computer types out the best possible shape for the pillar and the strength the pillar will have. The resulting posts are thin enough to allow visibility, sharply raked for style, shaped to keep road dirt from creeping off the screen onto the side windows, yet stoutly ready to protect the occupants in a crash.

The looks of the 350SL are a matter of taste, as always. Odds are that when you look at the car your reaction will be along the lines of "Ah, the new Mercedes-Benz." The stylists have achieved two important things. The 350SL is obviously a Mercedes-Benz and obviously new.

What the stylists also did was present a car that looks larger and heavier. Square corners and sharp angles contribute to this, and the sides of the body remain slabs, despite the fluting between the wheel openings. The car *is* bigger and heavier, so the failure to disguise this is an honorable one. Subjectively, the 230-280SL was more attractive.

Suspension and Brakes

THE MAJOR improvements enter here. The 350SL gets Mercedes' newest and best front and rear suspension, introduced on the 250-series sedan in 1968. The front system is conventional, i.e. upper and lower A-arms, tubular shock absorbers, coil springs, and is not all that different from earlier Mercedes IFS except that it incorporates anti-brake dive and doesn't need lubrication.

The rear suspension replaces Mercedes' low-pivot swing axle with semi-trailing arms, to give equal ride comfort and a much improved wheel geometry. Both are clearly superior to the suspensions on the 230-280SL. The factory simply couldn't make the change until there was a new frame on which to attach the components.

There are anti-roll bars at both ends, for roll resistance and ride comfort. Something new in shock absorbers: there are rubber bushings fitted to the shafts, to serve as low-rate bump stops. Mercedes describes them as auxiliary springs, on the grounds that they stiffen the ride before reaching full jounce.

The steering is Mercedes' familiar (and excellent) recirculating ball, with power assist as standard. The longer wheelbase results in a fractionally larger turning radius, up from 33.5 ft to 33.9.

Brakes are all disc, in effect a running change incorporated when the 250SL appeared. But the 350SL gets the ventilated front rotors used all around on the larger sedans, for cooling purposes. A power booster is standard.

Appointments and Interior

WHEN MERCEDES says two seats, Mercedes means just that. Driver and passenger each have a very separate half of the compartment, divided by a high console containing many of the myriad controls. Those two people are, however, catered to in every imaginable way, and then some.

Comfortable seat belts, for instance, begin at the floor pan. The section beneath the seats is structured for extra strength, enough to withstand the weight of person and seat in a crash. The seat frame is attached to the pan with equal care. The lap belts are part of the seat, with an inertia reel. The belt therefore always fits the wearer at the approved angle, and never need be adjusted. A shoulder strap isn't required for open cars, but the 350SL has one, also with an inertia reel. The shoulder belt attaches to the body side behind the seat and joins the lefthand lap belt, for a 3-point system that won't tangle, doesn't need adjustment and can be fastened

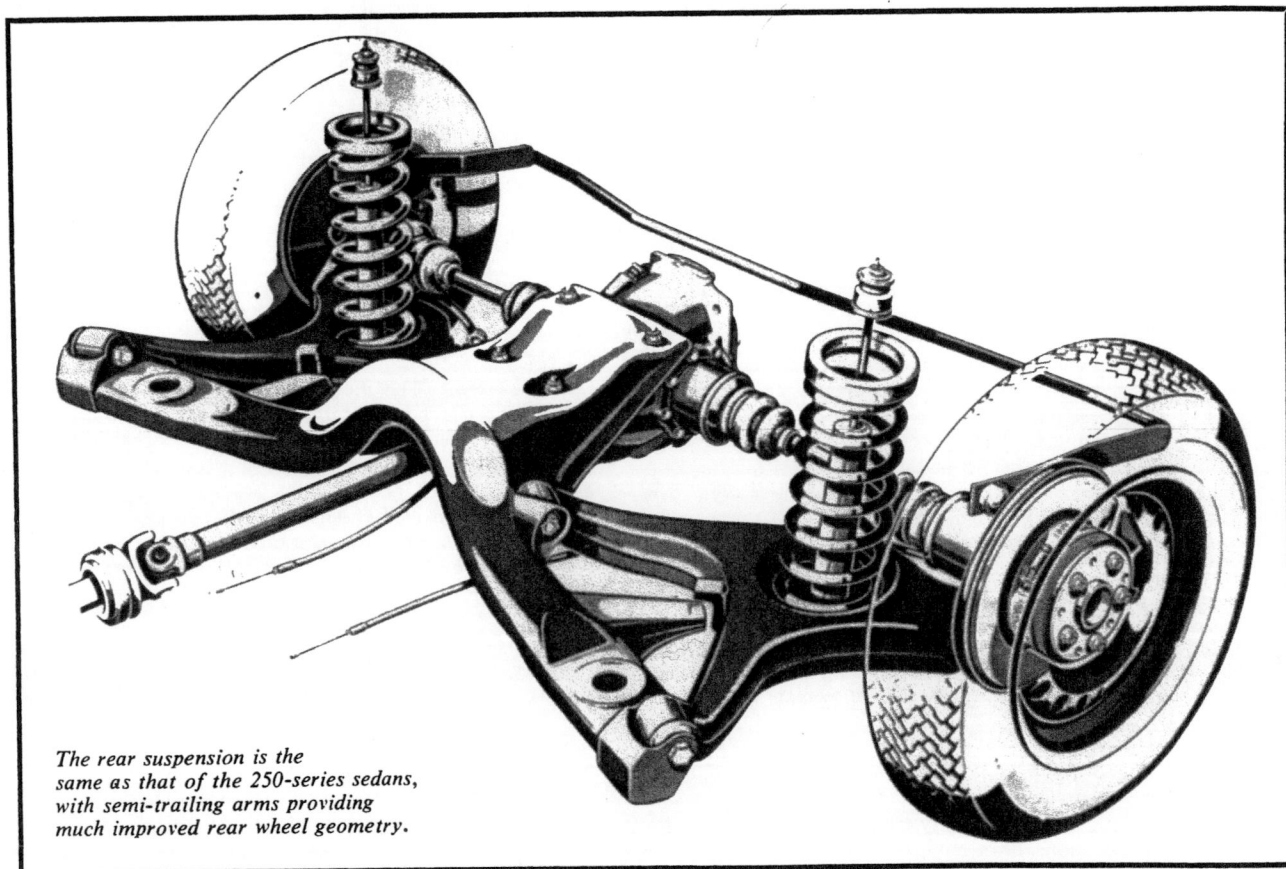

The rear suspension is the same as that of the 250-series sedans, with semi-trailing arms providing much improved rear wheel geometry.

MERCEDES·BENZ 350SL 4.5

or unfastened with one hand.

The seats themselves are typical Mercedes, carefully shaped with provision for height and fore-and-aft adjustment, and for seatback angle.

The inlets for the heat-ventilation system were placed in aerodynamically neutral areas of the body, so air flow doesn't vary with the speed of the car.

Under safety, Mercedes lists Europe's first remote-control outside mirror, padded dash and steering wheel, and an exterior door handle with no release knob. The handle must be pulled outward to reduce the risk of the door being opened by a blow. The hood pivots at the rear, so that in a frontal crash it will strike the windshield flat side to, rather than be rammed edge first into the passenger compartment.

The home-market cars have halogen headlights, halogen fog lights and an extra high-intensity bulb in the left taillight. This comes on when the foglights are in use and serves as a warning light for following cars. The U.S. version has SAE-standard headlights, foglights where the several states permit and no rear running light. When *are* we going to get a DOT lighting standard that incorporates the present?

Two of the 350SL's interior features border on the superfluous. The insides of the doors are both warmed and cooled by the heater/ventilation system, and there's a flashlight in the glovebox which plugs into the car's electrical system so as to be trickle charging when not in use.

Availability

As a 1972 car, the 350SL is not being rushed into U.S. delivery. First, the German dealers must be mollified, with one 350SL each, and then the certification tests must be run. Mercedes knows the car will pass but still, the form must be followed. So look for a price of about $10,000 and showroom introduction the first week of August.

Driving Impression

CIRCUMSTANCES PREVENT my having even a final preliminary report, so to speak. Press day for the 350SL was actually the introduction of the European version only and there were no 350SL 4.5s there. Or built yet, even. And the showing was at the Hockenheim race track, a lovely circuit but lacking (understandably) in the sort of bad pavement that separates the typical Mercedes from the typical car.

The engine size doesn't really matter. The 350SL engine will develop 230 gross horsepower in either 3.5- or 4.5-liter forms, so performance of the two versions should be nearly identical. At the end of the long straight, the display car was doing an indicated 120 mph, with more to come. The factory says top speed will be 130 and I have no grounds to doubt it. There may be some caution in the factory figures. I have been checking the performance of the 280SE 3.5 against the 280SL, and my guess is that the 350SL, with equal power and less weight than the sedan, will beat the official figure of 8.8 sec to 60 mph. More important, the bigger and heavier replacement will be quicker than the 280SL.

The suspension is a clear gain. One of the 280SL's more apparent flaws was extreme forward dive under braking. The use of the newer suspension reduces the dive by half, to what has become the norm. There was a surprising degree of squat under power. Engineering Director Rudolf Uhlenhaut (Cries of Name Dropper!) said this was a compromise. Selection of optimum ride rates and suspension geometry for the best possible ride and handling had the side effect of squat during acceleration. Small loss, he said rightly.

One could simply fill the appropriate handling blanks As you'd expect, the 350SL is very stable at speed, extremely comfortable and develops high cornering powers through fast corners and slow. The attitude is that of mild-but-obdurate understeer. The car can be forced to plow, but it's virtually impossible to break the rear end loose. One quirk: reducing power at the entrance to a turn pitches the tail out to the limit of spring travel. Disconcerting at first, but Uhlenhaut said—again rightly—that this would only show up at full speed on a track while the car was designed to be driven briskly on the proper half of public roads. However, Uhlenhaut gave me a ride around in his 350SL, fitted with stiff suspension and racing tires by the way, and he uses this initial yaw to position the car in the corner, said position being maintained through the curve by application of power. I don't think Mercedes designs cars by committee.

Inside, the 350SL simply feels right. Everything fits, from brake pedal to safety harness. I have a theory that good design is readily understood design, and every control worked as anticipated. Despite the handicaps mentioned earlier, the 350SL is a better car than its predecessor. —*Allan Girdler*

MERCEDES-BENZ 350SL 4.5 SPECIFICATIONS

Engine:
Type....................90 deg V-8, sohc
Bore x stroke, mm..........92.0 x 84.7
  Equivalent in...............3.62 x 3.33
Displacement, cc/cu in.........4500/275
Bhp.................................230
Fuel injection............Bosch electronic
Emission control..........engine mods
Drive Train:
Transmission.........3-speed automatic
  with torque converter

Chassis & Body:
Body/frame...................unit steel
Brake type: Ventilated disc front, solid disc
  rear; power assisted
Wheels..............steel disc, 14 x 6½
Tires.............radial, 205/70 VR 14
Steering type..............recirculating
  ball, power assisted
Turning circle, ft..................33.9
Front suspension: unequal length A-arms,
  coil springs, tube shocks, anti-roll bar

Rear suspension: semi-trailing arms, coil
  springs, tube shocks, anti-roll bar
General:
Curb weight, lb....................3405
Wheelbase, in.......................96.9
Track, front rear..............57.2/56.7
Overall length.....................172.1
Width..............................70.5
Height.............................51.2
Fuel tank capacity, U.S. gal..........23.8
Trunk capacity, cu ft................8.9

Mercedes-Benz

W107 Series 380SL

Specifications

Engine(s):	116·960 and 116·962
Number of Cylinders:	8
Cylinder arrangement:	V-shaped 90°
Bore & Stroke:	88mm by 78·9mm
Displacement:	3839cc
Compression ratio:	8·3 to 1
Firing order:	1-5-4-8-6-3-7-2
Crankshaft bearings:	5
Valve arrangement:	Overhead/hydraulic lifters
Camshaft arrangement:	OHC, one per cylinder bank

Mercedes-Benz

W107 Series 450SL

Specifications

Engine:	117·982
Number of Cylinders:	8
Cylinder arrangement:	V-shaped 90°
Bore & Stroke:	92mm by 85mm
Displacement:	4520cc
Compression ratio:	8:1
Firing order:	1-5-4-8-6-3-7-2
Crankshaft bearings:	5
Valve arrangement:	Overhead/hydraulic tappets From 1976 with Continuous Injections System (CIS)
Camshaft arrangement:	OHC, one per cylinder bank

Mercedes-Benz

W107 Series 560SL

Specifications

Engine:	117·967
Number of Cylinders:	8
Cylinder arrangement:	V-shaped 90°
Bore & Stroke:	96·50mm by 94·80mm
Displacement:	5547cc
Compression ratio:	96·50 to 1
Firing order:	1-5-4-8-6-3-7-2
Crankshaft bearings:	5
Valve arrangement:	Overhead/hydraulic lifters
Camshaft arrangement:	OHC, one per cylinder bank

Mercedes-Benz
W107 Series SL and SLC

Model	Years of production	Chassis	Engine
Mercedes-Benz 450SL	1972 to 1975	107·044	117·982
Mercedes-Benz 450SL	1976 to 1980	107·044	117·985
Mercedes-Benz 450SLC	1973 to 1975	107·024	117·982
Mercedes-Benz 450SLC	1976 to 1980	107·024	117·985
Mercedes-Benz 380SL	1981 to 1981	107·045	116·960
Mercedes-Benz 380SL	1982 to 1985	107·045	116·962
Mercedes-Benz 380SLC	1981 to 1981	107·025	117·960
Mercedes-Benz 300SL	1987 to 1989	107·041	103·982
Mercedes-Benz 560SL	1986 to 1989	107·048	117·967

AUTO TEST

MERCEDES-BENZ 350SL Coupé-convertible

More Touring Than Sporting

AT-A-GLANCE:
New two-seater convertible with detachable hardtop; vee-8 engine smooth but rather fussy and lacking in low-speed torque. Excellent power steering, precise handling. Superb brakes. Comfortable ride and seating. Economy poor. A very safe and well-built car.

ALTHOUGH completely different from its 280SL predecessor, the new 350SL carries on the same role as a very comfortable convertible touring two-seater rather than as a sports car. Special attention has been paid to safety, and the car has a feeling of considerable strength and weight. It is in fact 2½cwt heavier than the 280SL, which absorbs quite a lot of the extra 30 bhp available from the slightly larger vee-8 engine fitted. Consequently considerably more fuel is used, but there are still useful gains in both speed in all four gears and in acceleration.

The 3½-litre vee-8 engine with Bosch electronic fuel injection is the same unit as is installed in the 280SE 3.5 saloon and fits neatly beneath the very wide bonnet. It is a more prompt starter, having less of the delay sometimes experienced with the mechanical fuel injection. There is a lot of fussy noise at low speeds, especially obtrusive if the car has to be turned round or manoeuvred. When well under way, the noise level is less marked, though the engine could never really be called quiet, in spite of having a viscous fan coupling. Mixture enrichment for cold starting is automatic and the driver is scarcely aware of any change in behaviour as the engine warms up and the mixture returns to normal.

Standard transmission is a four-speed gearbox with central remote-control change, but the test car had the optional Daimler-Benz automatic transmission, again having a central change lever with the same unusual semi-pear-shaped knob on top. For the American market the letters D, S and L are used for the three forward gear positions, standing for Drive, Slope and Low. British

The windscreen wipers park over-lapped on the passenger side. Fog lamps mounted beneath the bumper are standard

Seat upholstery is in plaited pvc, but leather is optional. The light inside the facia locker incorporates its own battery, which recharges from the car battery; it can be removed for use as a torch

The under-bonnet compartment is packed with machinery, but all items requiring routine attention have been located for easy access. The bonnet is rear hinged and self-supporting

market cars have the more intelligible 4,3,2 marking, with fully automatic operation in position 4. However, the transmission is somewhat stodgy and unresponsive when left to itself, and except at or near full throttle, it is reluctant to change down for hills taken at quite low speeds, while the vee-8 engine is surprisingly lacking in low-speed torque. There is quite a thud and jolt when drive is first selected from neutral or park, but thereafter the changes are generally quite smooth.

The selector has pleasantly easy and light movement in a straight line between 4 and 3, so it is no hardship to drop it back to 3, which makes the transmission much more eager to change down, as well as holding third. The maximum for a kickdown change from third to second is increased from 32 to 43 mph when the lever is in position 3 instead of 4, and the change-down on part throttle is proportionately more responsive as well. Similarly, when position 2 is selected, the transmission will kick down to bottom gear at full throttle right up to 23 mph, instead of a mere 9 mph if position 4 is selected. The handbook recommends that position 2 should be selected for repeated stop-start work, as in dense, slow-moving traffic.

There is no positive hold for bottom gear, but the maximum speed in first goes up from 28 mph—the change-up point on full

MERCEDES-BENZ 350SL (3,499 c.c.)

ACCELERATION

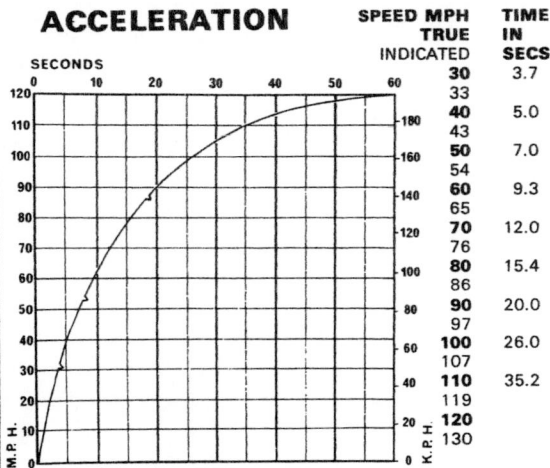

SPEED MPH TRUE INDICATED	TIME IN SECS
30	3.7
33	
40	5.0
43	
50	7.0
54	
60	9.3
65	
70	12.0
76	
80	15.4
86	
90	20.0
97	
100	26.0
107	
110	35.2
119	
120	
130	

GEAR RATIOS AND TIME IN SEC

mph	Top (3.46)	3rd (5.05)	2nd (8.27)
10- 30	—	—	3.6
20- 40	—	—	3.5
30- 50	8.3	5.7	3.8
40- 60	9.1	5.7	—
50- 70	9.7	5.6	—
60- 80	10.3	6.3	—
70- 90	11.2	8.4	—
80-100	12.2	—	—
90-110	15.2	—	—

Standing ¼-mile
17.0 sec 83 mph
Standing Kilometre
31.0 sec 105 mph
Test distance
743 miles
Mileage recorder accurate

PERFORMANCE

MAXIMUM SPEEDS

Gear	mph	kph	rpm
Top (mean)	126	203	6,500
(best)	126	203	6,500
3rd	87	140	6,500
2nd	53	85	6,500
1st	31	50	6,300

BRAKES

FADE
(from 70 mph in neutral)
Pedal load for 0.5g stops in lb

1	20-25	6	20-25	
2	20-25	7	20-25	
3	20-25	8	20-25	
4	20-25	9	20-25	
5	20-25	10	20-25	

RESPONSE
(from 30 mph in neutral)

Load	g	Distance
20lb	0.35	86 ft
40lb	0.72	42 ft
50lb	0.98	30.7ft
60lb	1.1	27.4ft
Handbrake	0.26	116ft
Max. Gradient	1 in 4	

COMPARISONS

MAXIMUM SPEED MPH

Aston Martin DBS 6-cyl	(£5,953)	140
Jaguar E-Type 2+2 6-cyl	(£2,979)	139
Jensen Interceptor	(£5,874)	137
BMW 3.0 CS	(£5,118)	131
Mercedes-Benz 350SL	(£5,457)	126

0-60 MPH, SEC

Jensen Interceptor	6.4
Jaguar E-Type 2+2	7.4
BMW 3.0 CS	8.0
Aston Martin DBS	8.6
Mercedes-Benz 350SL	9.3

STANDING ¼-MILE, SEC

Jensen Interceptor	15.0
Jaguar E-Type 2+2	15.4
BMW 3.0 CS	16.2
Aston Martin DBS	16.3
Mercedes-Benz 350SL	17.0

OVERALL MPG

BMW 3.0 CS	20.8
Jaguar E-Type 2+2	18.8
Mercedes-Benz 350SL	14.7
Jensen Interceptor	12.9
Aston Martin DBS	12.7

GEARING
(with 205/70-14 in. tyres)

Top	19.4 mph per 1,000rpm
3rd	13.3 mph per 1,000rpm
2nd	8.1 mph per 1,000rpm
1st	4.9 mph per 1,000rpm

CONSUMPTION

FUEL
(At constant speeds—makers' figures, mpg)

30 mph	32.2
40 mph	30.9
50 mph	28.1
60 mph	25.7
70.mph	23.0
80 mph	20.2
90 mph	17.7
100 mph	15.3

Typical mpg 15 (18.8 litres/100km)
Calculated (DIN) mpg
20.9 (13.5 litres/100km)
Overall mpg 14.7 (19.2 litres/100km)
Grade of fuel Premium- 4-star (min. 98RM)

OIL
Consumption (SAE30) 700 miles per pint

TEST CONDITIONS:
Weather: Dry, Sunny. Wind: 0-8 mph.
Temperature: 25 deg. C. (77 deg. F).
Barometer: 29.9 in. hg. Humidity: 50%
Surfaces: Dry. Concrete and asphalt.

WEIGHT:
Kerb Weight 30.4cwt (3,405lb-1,545kg).
(with oil, water and half full fuel tank).
Distribution, per cent F, 53.4; R, 46.6.
Laden as tested: 34.4cwt (3,853lb-1,748kg).

TURNING CIRCLES:
Between kerbs L, 32ft 0in; R, 33ft 5in.
Between walls L, 34ft 3in; R, 35ft 8in.
Steering wheel turns, lock to lock 3.3.
Figures taken at 1,700 miles by our own
staff at the Motor Industry Research
Association proving ground at Nuneaton
and on the Continent.

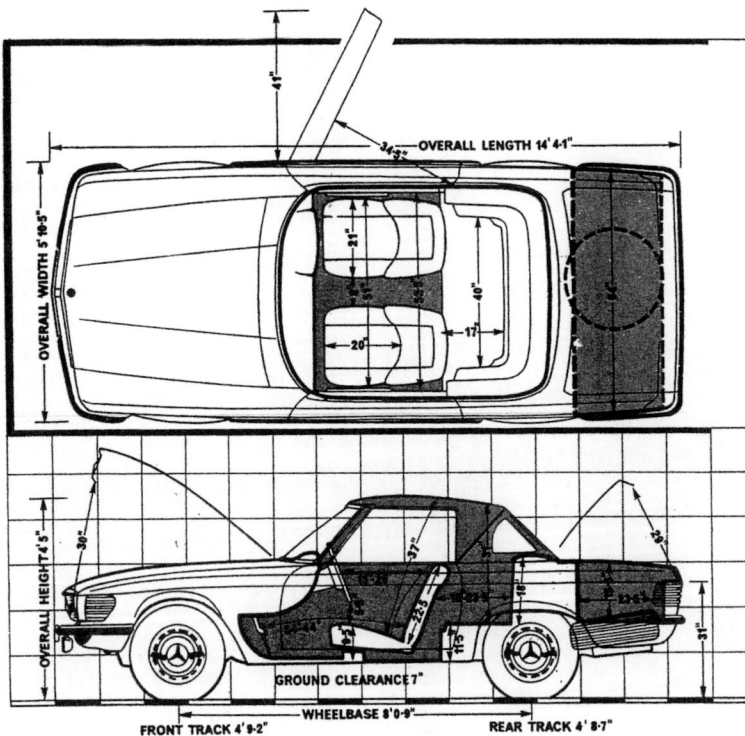

OVERALL LENGTH 14' 4·1"
OVERALL WIDTH 5' 10·5"
OVERALL HEIGHT 4' 5"
GROUND CLEARANCE 7"
WHEELBASE 8' 0·9"
FRONT TRACK 4' 9·2"
REAR TRACK 4' 8·7"
STANDARD GARAGE 16ft x 8ft 6in.

SPECIFICATION
FRONT ENGINE, REAR-WHEEL DRIVE
ENGINE

Cylinders	8, in 90 deg. vee
Main bearings	5
Cooling system	Water: pump, viscous-coupled fan, and thermostat
Bore	92mm (3.62in.)
Stroke	65.8mm (2.59in.)
Displacement	3,499 c.c. (213.5 cu.in.)
Valve gear	Single chain-driven overhead camshaft per bank, with finger followers
Compression ratio	9.5-to-1 Min. octane rating: 97
Carburation	Bosch electronic fuel injection
Fuel pump	Bosch electrical
Oil filter	Full flow, renewable element
Max. power	200 bhp (net) at 5,800 rpm
Max. torque	211 lb.ft (net) at 4,000 rpm

TRANSMISSION

Gearbox	Daimler-Benz 4-speed automatic with fluid coupling
Gear ratios	Top 1.0
	Third 1.46
	Second 2.39
	First 3.98
	Reverse 5.48
Final drive	Hypoid bevel, 3.46 to 1 (limited slip differential optional)

CHASSIS and BODY

Construction	Integral with steel body

SUSPENSION

Front	Independent: coil springs and wishbones with anti-dive geometry; progressive rubber helper springs. Telescopic dampers; anti-roll bar.
Rear	Independent: semi-trailing wishbones and coil springs; progressive rubber helper springs. Telescopic dampers; anti-roll bar.

STEERING

Type	Daimler-Benz power assisted, with automatic bleeding
Wheel dia	16.75in.

BRAKES

Make and type	Disc brakes all round, ventilated at front; separate inner brake drums for parking brake. Dual circuit hydraulic system
Servo	Vacuum servo standard
Dimensions	F10.75 in. dia. discs R11 in. dia. discs
Swept area	F 229 sq. in., R 201 sq. in. Total 430 sq. in. (250 sq. in./ton laden)

WHEELS

Type	Pressed steel disc 6½ in. wide rim
Tyres—make	Michelin
—type	X radial ply tubed
—size	205/70VR 14

EQUIPMENT

Battery	12 Volt 66 Ah.
Alternator	Bosch 490 watt 3-phase 55 amp
Headlamps	Bosch 90/80 watt (total)
Reversing lamps	Standard
Electric fuses	14
Screen wipers	Two-speed, with pause control
Screen washer	Standard, foot-operated with wipers
Interior heater	Standard, fresh air blending, separate left and right temp. controls
Heated backlight	Extra, available for Coupe only
Safety belts	Standard, inertia reel
Interior trim	Deep-embossed PVC seats, PVC head-lining
Floor covering	Carpet
Jack	Screw pillar with geared handle
Jacking points	Two each side under sills
Windscreen	Laminated
Underbody protection	PVC on surfaces exposed to road

MAINTENANCE

Fuel tank	19.8 Imp gallons (90 litres) (no reserve)
Cooling system	25 pints (including heater)
Engine sump	13.2 pints (7.5 litres) SAE 30. Change oil every 6,000 miles. Change filter element every 6,000 miles
Automatic transmission	10.2 pints ATF. Change oil every 30,000 miles
Final drive	2.5 pints SAE 90EP. Change oil every 12,000 miles
Grease	None required
Tyre pressures	F30; R 36 psi (normal driving) F 32; R 38 psi (fast driving)
Max. payload	430 kg (750 lb)

PERFORMANCE DATA

Top gear mph per 1,000 rpm	19.4
Mean piston speed at max. power	2,500 ft/min.
Bhp per ton laden	116

AUTOTEST
MERCEDES-BENZ
350 SL . . .

throttle—to 31 mph when the lever is at position 2. There is positive hold of both second and third gears to the recommended rev limit of 6,500 rpm, giving 53 mph in second and a commendable 87 mph maximum in third. Those who know the 280SL will find the gear ratios of the 350SL much improved, and the car is also more reasonably geared in top, now giving nearly 20 mph per 1,000 rpm. The rev limit can be reached in top gear, giving a maximum speed of 126 mph; but for ordinary fast cruising the car still seems somewhat under-geared, taking a little more than 5,000 rpm to sustain 100 mph.

The effects of low gearing and considerable weight also show up in the rather disappointing fuel consumption. None of the intermediate checks during the test reached even 16 mpg, with 15 mpg as the normal touring consumption on 4-star premium. Tank capacity is a generous 19.8 gallons, giving a normal range of some 250 miles with a couple of gallons in reserve before refuelling.

When we took the performance figures the car had still covered under 2,000 miles and would perhaps improve with further mileage, but it was able to accelerate from rest to 60 mph in 9.3sec, which is only slightly slower than the maker's claimed figure, while the rest to 100 mph time of 26.0sec represents a useful saving of 4.6sec against the 280SL.

Optional before, power-assisted steering is standard, and it responds extremely well so that drivers are hardly aware of the assistance except for the lack of effort needed at the wheel. In a straight line the steering accuracy is very good, with fine and progressive response to small corrections. On corners the car feels

very manageable, definitely with all four wheels planted firmly on the road, and with very little roll. The car is very well balanced and what little understeer there is gets disguised by the power steering, making the car handle very neatly and responsively on twisting roads.

The tendency to tail swing, and transition to oversteer when cornering really hard which used to be experienced with previous SLs, has been eliminated by the change to the more advanced independent rear suspension with semi-trailing links as on the "New Generation" saloons, instead of the low-pivot swing axle layout.

The steering wheel itself has a covering of perforated pvc on a padded rim, quite pleasant to feel and with recessed finger-tip horn pads at each edge of the wide central boss.

On ordinary roads the suspension feels surprisingly taut and firm, giving a rather lively ride, but there is no jar or harshness on bad bumps. As often happens, the suspension seems to soften up at speed, giving a level, well-damped and very comfortable ride. Comfort is enhanced by the well-contoured seats which give good lateral location, extend well forward under the thighs, and prove a good deal softer than is often the case with Mercedes seats. A knurled hand wheel at the outer edge of each gives progressive backrest adjustment.

Although the driver sits fairly high and has a good forward view over the flat bonnet, the considerable width is a slight embarrassment in confined spaces. Windscreen pillars are reasonably slim, and the side windows, raised by numerous turns of rather stiff winding handles, nestle neatly against the rubber seal without any awkward quarter vents.

The instruments can be seen clearly through the upper part of the steering wheel, and their glasses are sloped to eliminate reflections; this is so effective that they appear at first to have no glass. The large central speedometer has figures only at 20 mph intervals, and is flanked by a smaller diameter rev counter and a

Rubber facings to the front and rear bumpers are continued along the sides of the car to protect against carelessly opened car doors. The rubber-floored boot is a usefully deep compartment and the spare wheel is stowed beneath a moulded section of the floor, which hinges upwards for access

matching dial on the left containing the fuel, oil and temperature gauges. In a straight line beneath the instruments are warning tell-tales for the indicators, brake fluid and handbrake, ignition, and headlamps main beam. The fuel warning tell-tale is set in the fuel gauge. A touch button beneath the speedometer gives instant trip reset.

The already good ventilation has been further refined and when the doors are closed, air ducts line up to take air from the heater into the doors, giving radiated warmth to the interior and demisting the side windows. Four vertical travel levers adjust heater output, two of them regulating temperature individually for the left and right sides of the car. The third lever progressively opens the air inlet and the fourth one controls foot level air outlet. There are no fewer than four "eye-ball" outlets for cool air; two in the centre of the facia, either side of the clock, and one at each end, with three sliding lever regulators (one for the centre pair). In hot weather there is a welcome delivery of cool air assisted by the quiet three-speed fan, appreciated even with the hood down.

Particularly when new, it was quite a struggle to put up the hood of the 280SL, but the process is much imroved on the 350SL by provision of a lever-operated tensioner for the rear attachment of the hood. It can thus be fastened to the top of the screen first, using the two detachable levers provided, and then the back of the hood can be tensioned by turning the lever at the side of the luggage well behind the passenger seat. A wire across the rear window takes the tension up to the back bar of the hood frame, so that the material is not unduly stretched.

As before, the hood folds neatly away into a well with a hinged, rigid cover. A small lever inside the tensioning lever should release the hood tension, allowing the cover to be unlocked and hinged back; on the test car this was not working properly and we had some difficulty in releasing both the hood and the hardtop on a number of occasions. When the hardtop is fitted (Coupé-convertible model), it is recommended that the hood be removed from the car and stored separately during the winter in a cover which can be obtained for it. A heated rear window for the hardtop is optional. When the hardtop is on, ventilation extraction is through vents under the rear window.

With the hood down, the occupants are well protected by the screen and side windows, and not subjected to much buffeting, nor is wind noise excessive. The snug fit of the hood when raised eliminates draughts and wind whistle and the chief gains of the hardtop are greater security and improved visibility on the rear quarters. Hardtop removal is a job for two strong men. The car is also available without hardtop, as the Roadster, at £215 less.

Safety features include progressively crushable front and rear body sections, the familiar Mercedes impact breakaway mounting for the interior mirror, and recessing of door handles and even the bonnet release handle.

Firmly padded lips protect against injury from the facia. The Bosch headlamps have tungsten bulbs and give brilliant night-driving illumination with quite a sharp cut-off when dipped, and fog lamps are a standard fitting, turned on by pulling out the lighting switch to its first position. Pulled out to the second position, the switch turns on a brighter tail lamp on the offside, for use in fog. Left and right parking lamps are standard.

Under the general safety heading come also the 350SL's outstandingly good brakes. There is very strong servo assistance, and efficiency is excellent in return for exceptionally light loads on the sensibly wide brake pedal. Only 60lb effort on the pedal gives a 1.1g stop, and during fade testing there was no change at all in the unusually low 20-25lb pedal effort needed for $\frac{1}{2}$g deceleration from 70 mph, although considerable brake smell was noticed towards the end of the test. In contrast, the parking brake could not be persuaded on hard enough to secure the car on 1 in 3.

Mirror adjustable from inside

A usefully large door mirror is fitted, with an interior toggle lever enabling it to be adjusted from the driving seat with the window closed. To the rear of the transmission lever, on the centre of the console, is a press-down hazard warning lamp switch, to turn on all four of the huge flashing amber indicators.

Quite a spacious glove locker is provided in the left of the facia, and as well as locking, it has a useful safeguard in that its release catch slides, and would fool any casual attempt to open it. The boot is spacious and its lid can be left unlocked when required. One key is supplied which fits all locks, and there is another with rounded head which works only the ignition and steering lock and door locks. As a safety measure, the exterior door handles pull out to open, eliminating risk of accidental door opening in a side impact. Safety belts are standard with inertia reels built into the side of the car, behind the doors. Normally they fasten to anchor points incorporated with the seats, but British safety legislation demands that separate anchorage points be provided, and this is done as standard, before delivery in UK.

Some may regret that Daimler-Benz have done away with the time-honoured clap hands windscreen wipers, but the new ones overlap on the passenger side, are not obstructive to forward vision when parked, and clear a large area of the screen. A small toggle switch in the multi-purpose lever control for dipping headlamps and working the indicators gives one to-and-back sweep of the wipers every two or three seconds, as well as slow and fast speeds. A floor-button simultaneously operates wiper and windscreen washers.

The Mercedes-Benz 350SL proved less exciting than was expected. Instead, the emphasis is on comfort, safety and functional efficiency. □

With a bit of a struggle, and a strong pull, the hard top can be lifted off. The hood is an improvement over the 280SL hood, in having transparent quarter panels, and it is easier to put up, as tensioning can be done after the attachment has been made to the windscreen, using the two detachable levers provided

MANUFACTURER:
Daimler-Benz AG, Stuttgart-Untertürkheim, West Germany.
UK CONCESSIONAIRES:
Mercedes-Benz (GB) Ltd, Great West Road, Brentford, Middlesex.
PRICES (in UK)

Basic	£4,364.00
Purchase Tax	£1,092.88
Seat belts	Standard
Total (in G.B.)	£5,456.88

EXTRA (inc. P.T.)

*Automatic transmission	£233.75

*Fitted to test car

PRICE AS TESTED	**£5,690.63**

THE SUPER LIGHT series of Mercedes two-seaters started with the Silver Arrow SLR eight-cylinder racers in the Moss and Fangio days nearly 20 years ago. Or even further back if your abacus goes back as far as the SSK. And if a 3405 lb. car can still qualify for a "super light" title, then the latest Mercedes 350SL two-seater still carries on the tradition.

There have been many transformations of the concept since the racing days. The gull-winged 300SL which followed them being the closest to a real competition car.

The rather tame but pretty 190 SL which followed drained the sporting appeal completely from the concept, replacing it with the future pattern, comfort, roadholding and brakes instead of brute, hairy power.

From the four-cylinder 190 SL to the six-cylinder 230 SL followed the pattern of the SL being a two-seater version of the sedan components — suspension included — which offered more style and a little more agility than its larger brethren.

The body of the 230 SL had hints of the gutsy 300SL days with its muscular looking mudguards and crisp styling lines. Its rather dainty pagoda roof — disputed by Italian Michelotti as to who first thought of it — distinguished it.

Successive engine enlargements took the car to the fuel injected 280 SL, a 124 mph, comfortable and solid tourer for two. Speed had gone up six mph, engine capacity half a litre and acceleration rather more than the figures suggest.

Available here with only automatic transmission, it was still available in Europe with four-speed transmission and a rumored five speed was also reputed to be "just around the corner" and certainly was under test.

Then came the 350SL. It is the epitome of what you can expect pollution and safety rules to do to a 300SL. Half a litre more, slower through much greater weight and styling for sales and safety appeal rather than pure aerodynamic needs.

But the evolution of the SL has been pacing demand in its market sector. There has never been a great shortage of customers in proportion to sedan and coupe sales.

It is intended for the sporting gentleman who sees no need to compromise comfort for performance. And that's how it comes out. Brisk, neatly precise from A to B and about as exciting as last week's suet.

It has many remarkable features however. Its motor for example meets the restrictive Californian emission tests — but requires another litre capacity to retain performance while doing this.

more ➡

MERCEDES
350 SL

KZB·500

SPECIFICATIONS

CAR FROM:
LANES MOTORS, Exhibition St., Melbourne

PRICE AS TESTED
$16,095

OPTIONS FITTED:
NONE

ENGINE:
Type ....V8, fuel injected, SOHC
Bore and Stroke ....92 x 66 mm
Capacity ....3499 cc
Compression ratio 9.5:1
Power ....200 bhp at 5800 rpm
Torque ....211 ft. lbs. at 4000 rpm.

TRANSMISSION:
Type ....Four speed automatic
Final drive 3.46:1

CHASSIS:
Wheelbase ....97 inches
Length ....172 inches
Track F ....57¾ inches
Track R ....56¼ inches
Width ....70½ inches
Height ....51¼ inches
Clearance (Minimum) ....7 inches
Test weight ....3405 lbs.
Fuel capacity ....19¾ gallons

SUSPENSION:
Front: Independent, coil springs and twin wishbone stabiliser bars.
Rear: Independent, coil springs and semi trailing wishbones, stabiliser bar.

BRAKES:
Power assisted, divided systems.
Front: Disc 10¾ in. diameter
Rear: Disc 11 in. diameter.

STEERING:
Type: Worm and sector, power assisted.
Turning circle: 33 ft.

WHEELS/TYRES:
14 in. steel, vented, finned and strengthened 6.5 in rims with 205 section radial ply tyres.

PERFORMANCE

Zero to
30 mph ....3.2 seconds
40 mph ....4.6 seconds
50 mph ....6.4 seconds
60 mph ....8.9 seconds
70 mph ....11.2 seconds
80 mph ....NA
90 mph ....NA
100 mph ....NA
Standing quarter mile 16.7 seconds.
Fuel consumption on test 14-19 mpg on super fuel.
Fuel consumption (expected) 16 mpg.
Cruising range 300 miles.
Speedometer error:

Indicated	30	40	50	60	70	80	90	100
Actual	29	39	49	59	69	79	NA	NA

MAXIMUM SPEEDS IN GEARS:
1st ....34 mph
2nd ....58 mph
3rd ....97 mph
4th ....126 mph

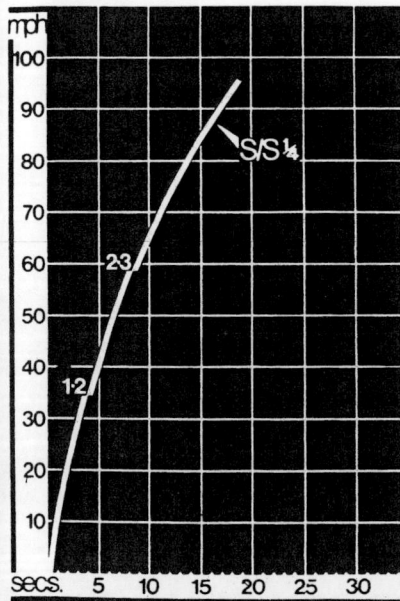

COMMENTS

ENGINE:
Response ....V good
Vibration ....Low
Noise ....Low

DRIVE TRAIN:
Shift linkage ....V good
Synchro action ....V good

STEERING:
Effort ....Light
Road feel ....Good
Kickback ....Nil

SUSPENSION:
Ride comfort ....V good
Roll resistance ....V good
Pitch control ....V good

HANDLING:
Directional control ....V good
Predictability ....V good

BRAKES:
Pedal pressure ....V low
Response ....V good
Fade resistance ....V good
Directional stability ....Excellent

CONTROLS:
Wheel position ....V good
Pedal position ....V good
Gearshift position ....Good

INTERIOR:
Front seat comfort ....V good
Front leg room ....V good
Front head room ....V good
Rear seat comfort ....V good
Rear leg room ....V good
Rear head room ....V good
Instrument legibility ....Excellent

VISION:
Forward ....Excellent
Front quarter........................Excellent
Rear ....Excellent

CONSTRUCTION QUALITY:
Paint ....V good
Chrome ....Good
Trim ....V good

GENERAL:
Headlights -- highbeam ..Fair to good
Headlights -- lowbeam ....Good
Parking/signal lights ....V good
Wiper coverage ....V good
Wipers at speed ....V good
Maintenance accessibility..Fair to good

In returning to eight cylinders, Mercedes have sounded a very faint echo to the days of the SLR Arrows. But the V8 today has mild camshaft timing attuned to stop and start traffic rather than the Routes Nationale and Autobahnen.

For 3499 cc, Mercedes have extracted a net 200 bhp. This is not stressing the motor unduly and to keep the motor smooth and efficient at its 6000 rpm maximum power point, single overhead camshafts with chain drives are used and fuel injection. Maximum torque is achieved at a quite high 4000 rpm.

That compares with America's 4.5 litre version of the same motor which, with a longer stroke, lower compression and milder cams produces 230 bhp (SAE) 5000 rpm and maximum torque at 3200 rpm. Torque figure is up in America from 211 to 279 ft. lbs. (performance effect is nil since they fit 3 speed auto, clean air gear and air-conditioning which removes the excess almost completely.)

And the 6.3 litre version which from 6329 cc gives 250 bhp at 4000 rpm and a huge 369 ft. lbs. torque at an even lower 2800 rpm.

It's how you slice it. Small and tweaky like the 3.5 or big and lazy like the 6.3. We'd like to see the 6.3 with tweaky bits in the 350 — now there's a 300SL successor if you like automatic transmission and air and all.

But the 350 SL, automatic transmission fitted as we get it in Australia, is no slouch off the mark. It's just that a chequered flag in the past keeps getting in our way.

Major change to the 350 SL — apart from new body and dash and interior and motor — is in the suspension. It now has the semi trailing wishbone and coil spring set-up from the compact 220 and 230/250 models.

It is a logical flow-on of design to have the smaller wheelbased cars in the range similarly suspended. The effect is extremely good on ride and driving qualities.

Brakes are vented front discs and solid rear discs of larger diameter with divided systems and power assistance.

Tyres are the fat 205 VR radial ply types with the 6.5 in. rimmed wheels having strengthening fluting behind the venting holes. These also create air turbulence over the brake discs and calipers' inside pistons.

The interior of the car — where the buyer is going to get his jollies for his $16,095 investment — is unspectacularly good and efficient. Nothing distracts from the excellent vision from the driver's seat.

But from the lower corner of the driver's eye can be seen the excellent new instruments, three large dials with a huge speedometer being flanked by the tachometer and a three needle and multi warning light combination instrument.

Water temperature, fuel contents and that rather negative oil pressure gauge Mercedes insist on. If the needle moves off the stop at 45 psi (assuming that really is 45 psi which I doubt after chatting with some instrument people) then all is not well with the motor. That comes into the category of a warning light which won't draw your attention. At idling speed, the oil pressure needle does a small dance to assure you it is functioning and not glued to the 45 stop.

For the increasing number of motorists bedevilled with speed limits, the huge speedometer with commendably clear calibration will be invaluable.

The styling of the 350 SL will either appeal or not depending on your taste but the stylists in Germany have done a fine job of blending in the American design rule sizes and heights with the European standards and making the final result quite palatable to the eye. The odd side window line comes from the hardtop's necessity to cover the capping for the soft top's compartment.

It certainly has a more meaty appearance than the faintly fragile but sleek lines of its predecessor.

Every time the starter is turned the motor fires and idles with a quiet V8 exhaust rumble. The fuel injection has no surges or hiccups and there's thankfully nothing mechanical for the driver to fiddle with to upset the machine. It just goes.

Selecting a gear with the sensibly gated floor lever for the automatic entails a slight delay while the transmission thinks about it and then gives you the gear, forward or reverse. This is part of the idiot-proof lockout which prevents you getting reverse at 80 mph — by accident.

The transmission is new in its interior works and starts in bottom gear rather than second for normal starting. The shift to second takes place unnoticed at about 10 mph.

Second to third comes about 25-30 mph and the shift into top requires a conscious lift off the pedal at 35 mph. It will go into top at 45 without provocation.

Using the lever to hold the middle two ratios — first just automatically changes to second at 34 mph — you get 58 mph in second and 97 mph in third. Using kickdown for overtaking, the V8's excess torque covers earlier shifting and performance isn't greatly different.

Gear shifts are smoother with the new transmission which seems to have a "looser" coupling or a higher stall speed. The effect is that the car won't wheelspin on maximum acceleration from rest on a dry road. There's very little squat from the rear either. Just a more noticeable whirring from the motor and plenty of bite.

From 0-50 mph took just 6.4 seconds, which is respectably fast. For 3.5 litres and 3400 lbs. It indicates the horses must all be on the job. The standing quarter mile time of 16.7 sec. comes fairly high in the 80's.

It's not a car designed for simply straight line work, however, and bends and long trips ferreted out its true nature. It is a very secure two seater touring car.

With the new suspension to keep rear wheel camber angle changes to a minimum, the car could be whisked through twisting roads with excellent roadholding and predictable if not inspiring handling.

The car took bends with a slight, designed-in understeer. Full power could alter the balance to neutral handling — but no further. The tail wouldn't come out. Soft spring rates possible with a two seater meant the wheels could roll out bumps in corners without the car losing its footing.

A glance at the interior would show just the type of market envisaged. Sedan seats, excellently shaped and proportioned with reclining backs, neat subdued carpeting, four nozzle cool air venting, individual temperature selection for air from the heater for each occupant, an efficient radio, superb vision all round and styling built to please government testers rather than aesthetics. Padding here, padding there, soft this, crushable that.

So rather than for a driver wishing to experience motoring's waning pleasures, the 350 SL is for one no longer interested in motoring but who likes efficient, comfortable transport with just a slight styling flair.

It is more 190 SL with optional sting than you might think. But on second thoughts, they weren't so bad either. There's still an awful lot of them about. They were well made as befits the three pointed star.

MERCEDES 450SL

*We've said it before
and it's still true:
the ultimate luxury 2-seater*

MERCEDES-BENZ INTRODUCED the 450SL in 1971 (at that time it was designated the 350SL 4.5) as a replacement for the 230–250–280 SL series of fast, open-closed, 2-seater luxury cars. The change from the 280SL to the newer model was a sweeping one even though the basic concept was the same for both cars. The 450SL is longer, wider and heavier and is marked by all-new styling featuring a subtle wedge shape. In the five years since its introduction, the new Mercedes has changed little in appearance and engineering outside of meeting increasingly tough U.S. safety and emission standards.

The styling is typical, conservative Mercedes-Benz with bulbous sides, a removable hardtop that retains just a bit of the concave look of the pagoda roof of the 280SL, and a rather unattractive upsweep to the rear quarter windows. The 450SL has a heavy look to it, testifying that it is a Mercedes: a solid and substantial machine, with clean and contemporary appearance and little crispness or agility, thank you anyway.

In any discussion of Mercedes' cars, three words always come to the forefront: luxury, comfort and handling. The 450SL has an abundance of all three. The interior appointments are precisely what you would expect, from the rather firm, fairly high off the floor and quite comfortable seats to the impressive instrumentation, highlighted by white-on-black gauges that are

easy to read and bespeak Teutonic efficiency. Our test car for this guide was equipped with the optional leather upholstery package and while the remainder of the interior appointments are one notch down from that, the overall effect is very pleasing.

The controls are perhaps the best worked-out of any car we've driven. The turn signal lever also operates the windshield wiper/washer system as well as dimming and raising the headlights. A new feature for the 450SL in 1976 is cruise control which is activated by a second stalk just above the turn signal lever to the left of the steering wheel. The seatbacks are infinitely adjustable by means of large round knobs on the inside edges and we liked the fact that the seatbacks pivot on a point several inches above the cushion to vary lumbar support as the back angle is changed. The heating and ventilation system is somewhat complex with separate heat controls for driver and passenger and color and light codes to tell one from another that require a certain amount of study of the owner's manual prior to operation.

In the changeover from the 280SL to the 450SL, Mercedes and the Behr company of Germany expended a considerable amount of energy to improve the air conditioning system. On the 280SL, it was a hang-on system with no provision for processing fresh air and was generally inadequate for American weather conditions. The newer system is built-in and uses fresh air except on the very coldest setting. The present compressor is the GM-Frigidaire swashplate unit, which must rank as the quietest, smoothest and most efficient compressor available today. The system feeds through the same ductwork as is used for the heater, delivering cooled air to four dash nozzles, the foot area or the windshield, or any combination of the three.

The 4.5-liter V-8 engine is very much like an American V-8 in behavior, both quiet and smooth running, with only a few reminders of mixture leaness to meet emission standards. The 450SL is available in the U.S. only with a 3-speed automatic transmission developed specifically for the 4.5-liter engine. Mercedes has traditionally built 4-speed automatics with fluid coupling, but because of the good low-speed torque of the big V-8, a 3-speed with torque converter was deemed adequate, and it is. The automatic is very smooth shifting and responds instantly to driver demands for downshifting, It has a gated

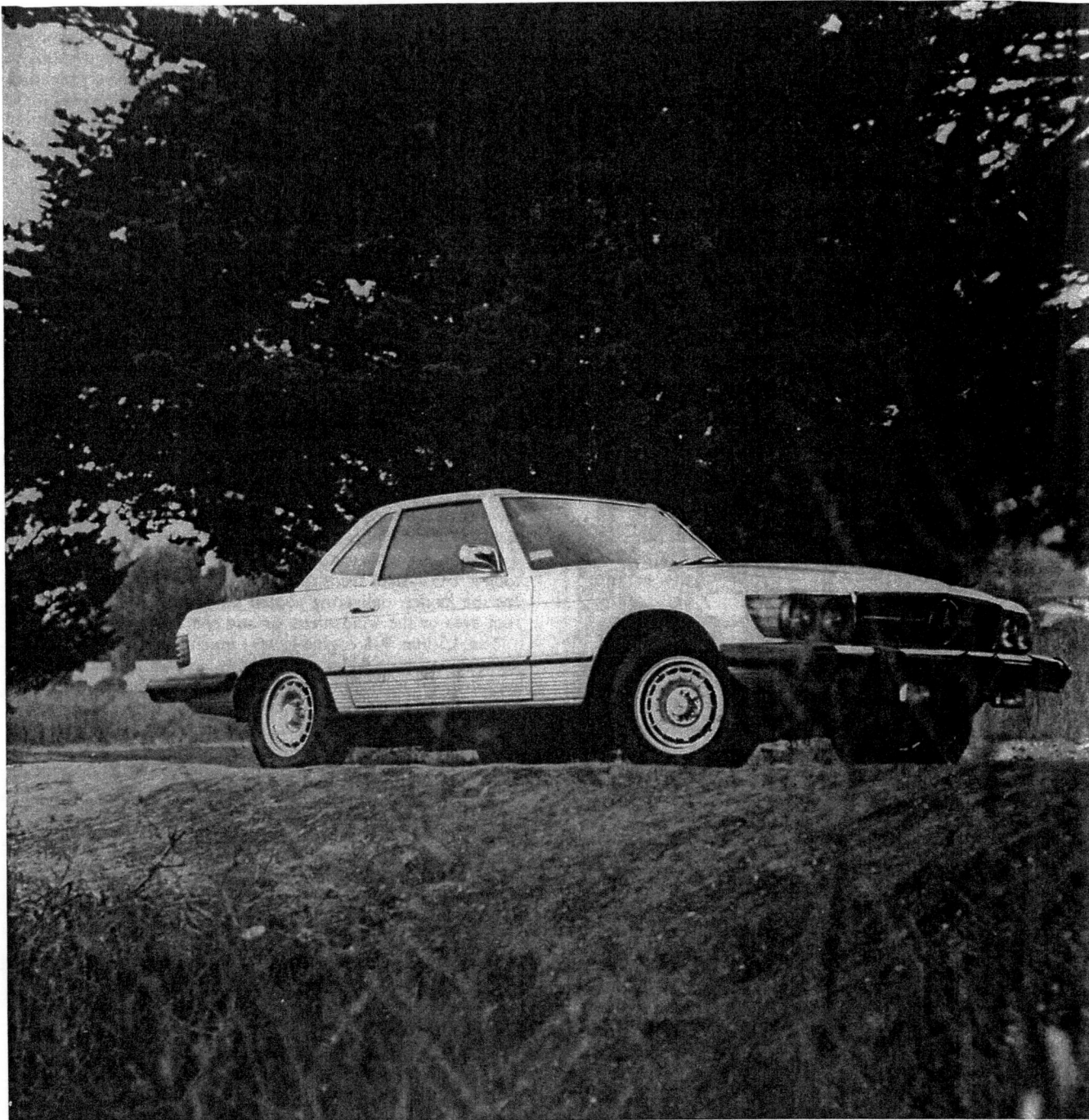

shift pattern which we like very much in an automatic as it prevents slipping into an inappropriate gear when shifting for yourself. The automatic does take away from the performance of the 450SL, however, and in fact the car is not as quick in acceleration as the 6-cylinder 280SL it replaced. Part of this is also attributable to the very tall gearing of the newer car which has a 3.07:1 final drive ratio that allows a high top speed and lower engine speeds during highway cruising.

While the newer car may not accelerate as quickly as the older 280SL, it has a clearcut advantage in the handling department. Gone is the 280SL's tendency of front-end squash during braking, thanks to angled A-arms that provide a moderate degree of anti-dive effect. Gone too are the rear swing axles, replaced by semi-trailing arms which keep rear wheel camber nearly ideal during cornering. The result of these changes is a car that is thoroughly modern in its handling: close to neutral with a small amount of understeer in nearly all conditions to stabilize things. It's still possible to bring the tail out by lifting

the throttle foot during hard turning, but the change is gentle and controllable.

The ride characteristics are exemplary. Monstrous dips and bumps can be taken at speed without fear of upsetting the car's aplomb. There is slightly more harshness over small surface irregularities at very low speeds than some might expect, but generally the 450SL can be driven fast over any road surface while the excellent chassis and rattle-free body take care of things. On smooth surfaces, the ride is uncanny: very little harshness, minimal pitching and no roll to speak of.

The standard power steering merits an excellent rating too for its responsiveness and crispness. Its road feel is close to perfect and there is a very good reason for this: the amount of effort at the steering wheel is absolutely proportional to the effort at the tires. The larger-than-average steering wheel is a feature we like very much, as it inspires confidence in fast corners and gives most drivers a feeling of ease in controlling the car's direction.

It should come as no surprise that the braking is also very good. It's been years since a Mercedes exhibited any fade in our testing and the 450SL is no exception. The ventilated front discs will lock up if the driver keeps his foot jammed on during a panic stop but the car will maintain the proper attitude and direction and it's unlikely any driver will experience panic in an emergency situation driving this car.

There is a slightly larger version of the car, the 450SLC, which has room for four adults in surprising comfort. The larger car is some 14 in. longer and has a slightly higher roofline. It shares the same drivetrain, suspension and front body panels with the 450SL, but it is a separate car that was developed along with the smaller Mercedes and is not simply a stretched version. Its greater overall length and increased wheelbase give it a slightly better ride, the handling is also quite good and performance does not suffer to any great degree despite the 150-lb weight differential. The 450SLC is strictly a coupe with no provision for removing the top as with the 450SL, which has both hard and soft tops. The aesthetics of the two cars are subjective to some degree, but to us the SLC version is not as well proportioned as the SL, which we find compact and clean.

After an earlier test, we concluded the report on the 450SL with these words: "In summary, the 450SL is the ultimate in a 2-seat luxury car. Its great weight, luxury equipment and mandatory automatic transmission keep it from being a sports car or an entertainment machine, but if one desires merely to drive fast in supreme comfort and avoid the clumsiness of a big sedan, there is no better choice than the 450SL." The intervening three years have not changed that opinion. ⊕

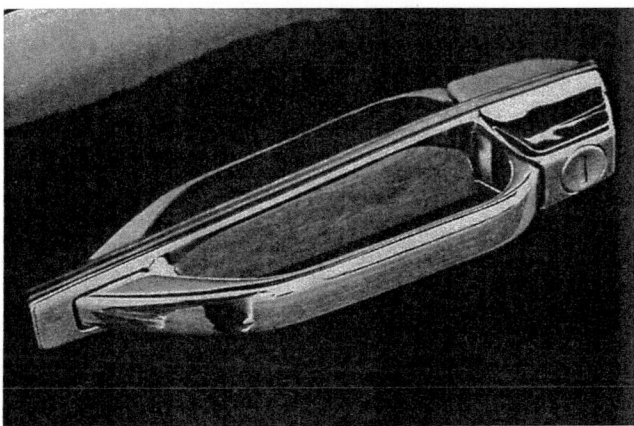

MERCEDES 450SL

PRICE
List price, west coast $18,330
Price as tested $18,930

GENERAL
Curb weight, lb 3780
Test weight 4005
Weight distribution (with driver),
  front/rear, %.................. 56/44
Wheelbase, in 96.9
Track, front/rear 57.2/56.7
Length 182.3
Width 70.5
Height 51.2
Ground clearance...................... 5.3
Overhang, front/rear 37.5/47.6
Usable trunk space, cu ft........ 14.5
Fuel capacity, U.S. gal 23.8

ENGINE
Type .... sohc V-8
Bore x stroke, mm ....91.9 x 85.1
  Equivalent in..........3.62 x 3.35
Displacement, cc/cu in.. 4520/276
Compression ratio 8.0:1
Bhp @ rpm, net.......180 @ 4750
  Equivalent mph................... 111
Torque @ rpm, lb-ft..220 @ 3000
Fuel injection....... Bosch electronic
Fuel requirement.. 91-oct unleaded

DRIVETRAIN
Transmission: automatic; torque
  converter with 3-speed planetary
  gearbox
Gear ratios: 3rd (1.00) 3.07:1
  2nd (1.46)...................... 4.49:1
  1st (2.31) 7.10:1
  1st (2.31 x 2.00)............ 14.20:1
Final drive ratio................... 3.07:1

CHASSIS & BODY
Layout ....front engine/rear drive
Body/frame .... unit steel
Brake system: 10.8-in. vented disc
  front, 11.0-in. solid disc rear;
  vacuum assisted
Brake swept area, sq in 421
Wheels .... 14 x 6½
Tires .... 205/70 VR 14
Steering type: recirculating ball,
  power assisted
Overall ratio...................... 15.9:1
Turns, lock-to-lock 3.0

Turning circle, ft 33.9
Front suspension: unequal-length
  A-arms, coil springs, tube shocks,
  anti-roll bar
Rear suspension: semi-trailing arms,
  coil springs, tube shocks, anti-
  roll bar

INSTRUMENTATION
Instruments: 160-mph speedo,
  7000-rpm tach, odo, trip odo, oil
  pressure, coolant temp, fuel level,
  clock

ROAD TEST RESULTS

ACCELERATION
Time to distance, sec:
  Standing ¼-mi, sec........... 18.4
  Speed at end, mph 82
Time to speed, sec:
  0–30 mph 4.8
  0–50 mph 8.5
  0–60 mph 10.9
  0–70 mph 14.3
  0–80 mph 18.0

SPEED IN GEARS
3rd gear (5075 rpm) 117
2nd (5800) 96
1st (5800)............................. 61

FUEL ECONOMY
Normal driving, mpg............... 16.5
Cruising range (1-gal. res) 375

HANDLING
Speed on 100-ft radius, mph .. 32.4
Lateral acceleration, g 0.700

BRAKES
Minimum stopping distances, ft:
  From 60 mph 184
  From 80 mph 302
Overall brake rating ...... very good

SPEEDOMETER ERROR
30 mph indicated is actually 27
50 mph 48
60 mph 58
70 mph 68
80 mph 77
90 mph 87
Odometer, 10.0 mi.................. 9.8

MERCEDES-BENZ 380 SLC

Mercedes' 3.8 litre all-alloy V8 mated to a new four-speed automatic gearbox gives the SLC two-door coupé good performance and economy, but after eight years in production is this sleek grand tourer beginning to show its age? Read on . . .

IT IS no secret that many people had expected the new Mercedes-Benz range of two-door SL and SLC sports cars, introduced at last year's Geneva Show, to reflect the styling and aerodynamic changes incorporated in the new 'S' class saloons. Indeed, the current body shape has gone unchanged since 1972 and although it has that classic 'carved from solid' appearance, to many eyes it is beginning to look dated.

Yet despite this, sales of the drop-head SL and coupé-bodied SLC in Britain at least have actually increased during the past 12 months with 686 SLs being sold (504 in 1979) and 471 SLCs (421). So until the new model range arrives, it looks as though the current cars will continue to attract a small band of well-heeled buyers.

The revisions to the existing range came about with the introduction of the new all-alloy 90-degree V8 for the 'S' class saloons. The engine is available in two sizes: 3,818 cc, which is fitted to the 380 SL and 380 SLC (the subject of this test) and replaces the old 450 unit; and 4,973 cc which, for the British market, is surprisingly available only in the 500 SL. The 280 SL and SLC models have the 2,746 cc six-cylinder, twin overhead camshaft fuel-injected engines already in use in the 280 SE and 280 E saloons and 280 CE coupé. This engine replaces the 350-series units.

Both the 380 and the slingshot 500 models drive their rear wheels via a new Mercedes-built all-hydraulic 4-speed automatic gearbox (manual transmission is no longer available on these models) while the well-proven suspension (double wishbones and coil springs at the front and semi-trailing arms and coil springs at the rear with an anti-roll bar at each end) is unchanged. Slight modifications, though, have been made to the front wishbones to accommodate modified brake calipers with bigger pads to extend their life, and at the rear there is now anti-squat geometry to prevent the tail from dipping under hard acceleration.

Outwardly, the cars are little changed. The SL and SLC now have a plastic foam bib air dam under the front bumper, said to reduce drag by five per cent and front end lift by no less than 30 per cent. Despite these improvements (the 500 SL also has a small boot spoiler), the revised sports cars cannot match the 0.36 drag coefficient of the new 'S' class saloons.

At £21,531, the two-door 380 SLC (Sports Light Coupé) is far from cheap, being close to the top end of the luxury sports coupé market. The strong value of the pound, though, has allowed Mercedes-Benz to include a long list of standard equipment, normally only available at extra cost. Nevertheless, the Mercedes has some strong rivals in the shape of the Jaguar XJS (£19,187), the BMW 635 CSi Auto (£18,950), the Porsche 928 Auto (£21,827), the Lotus Elite 2.2 Auto (£17,137) and the Ferrari 308 GT4 (£17,534), soon to be replaced by the new Ferrari Mondiale, expected to cost around £25,000.

PERFORMANCE

★★★★ The all-alloy 3,818 cc V8 engine has a single overhead cam-shaft for each bank of cylinders and is no less than 100 lb lighter than its predecessor. With a compression ratio of 9.0:1 and induction by Bosch K-Jetronic mechanical injection (Mercedes-Benz still distrust electronic systems), maximum power is 218 bhp (DIN) at 5,500 rpm. This is 1 bhp more than the larger 450 engine developed, but maximum torque is down from 271 to 224 lb ft, peaking at 4,000 rpm instead of 3,250 rpm.

Because of the reduction in overall weight (close to 2.3 cwt compared with the 450 SLC we tested w/e May 1 1976), slightly improved aerodynamics and a gearbox which allows more efficient use of the engine, the 380 SLC is a close match in performance to its predecessor, despite the loss of torque.

From standstill, the 380 will reach 60 mph in 8.4 sec and 100 mph in 23.0 sec whereas the 450 recorded times of 8.5 sec and 22.4 sec respectively. With the full-throttle change-up points on the four-speed automatic gearbox designed to keep the tachometer needle in the optimum torque range, we found there was little to be gained in holding the changes manually.

Unless most of your driving is done in town, standing starts are of limited interest, more important is the mid-range performance. In kickdown the 380 will accelerate from 30-50 mph in a creditable 3.1 sec (3.3 sec for the 450) and 50-70 mph in 4.9 sec (4.5 sec). Good as these figures seem, they are by no means exceptional for the class with most of the Mercedes' rivals being considerably quicker, particularly the less-expensive Jaguar XJS which will accelerate from 0-60 mph in 7.6 sec and cover the 50-70 mph increment in 3.5 sec.

Unfortunately we were unable to verify Mercedes top speed claim of 133 mph, but the ease with which 130 mph could be summoned — even within the confines of MIRA — suggests that the figure is if anything on the conservative side with 135 mph being closer to the mark.

Throughout our test the 380 rarely failed to start from cold at the first turn of the key and would warm quickly and without hesitations. At tickover, the engine is almost inaudible and on the move settles to a deep, satisfying V8 throb. Even when pressed the engine note is restrained and a cruising speed of 110-120 mph is quite feasible in spite of fairly low gearing which has the engine spinning at 4,500 rpm at 100 mph.

ECONOMY

★★ ★★ It would be fair to say that anyone who buys a £21,000 performance coupé is likely to be less interested in fuel economy than the average driver, but they should be well-pleased with the 380's thirst. Despite our usual hard driving (including no less than three visits to MIRA for performance testing) the car returned 16.7 mpg overall; we estimate the average owner would easily achieve 19 mpg and possibly as much as 21 or 22 mpg. Our overall figure is above average for the class, bettering those of the Jaguar (13.5 mpg), the Ferrari (14.1 mpg) and the BMW manual (16.5 mpg) as well as the previous 450 SLC (15.1 mpg), but is below the Porsche 928 Auto's 18.5 mpg. The figure is even more creditable considering the rather low overall gearing (22.3 mph/1000 rpm), which is aimed more at performance than economy.

On a full 19.8 gallon tank of four-star petrol (including a 2.8 gallon reserve), a range of over 390 miles should be within easy reach. Although the tank fills easily to the brim, the heavy-spring loading of the fuel filler flap, which opens from the top, makes filling a two-handed operation.

TRANSMISSION

★★ ★ Improved fuel consumption was one of the prime objectives Mercedes had in designing the new automatic gearbox, the other being good cost-effectiveness in production. Improvements to the torque converter is one of several modifications which have reduced mechanical losses to almost two-thirds of those in previous 'boxes.

The first application of the new four-speed transmission was in the 'S' class saloons and gained considerable praise when tested in the 380 SEL saloon (Motor w/e October 4 1980). Despite having a similar gearbox with identical ratios and final drive, we were disappointed with its application in the 380 SLC.

In 'Drive', all four forward gears are available (in 'D' the bigger-engined 500 starts off in second), but unlike the saloon, first to second and second to third changes are particularly lumpy unless full throttle is used. Closing the throttle after hard acceleration also results in an uncomfortably jerky change.

Although to its credit the kickdown into 3rd is commendably responsive both on part- and full-throttle, the SLC's transmission proved reluctant to kickdown into 2nd even at very low road speeds, this being particularly annoying when you wish to accelerate quickly out of a roundabout.

On full-throttle acceleration from rest, the gearbox will change from first to second at 4,900 rpm (29 mph), into third at around 5,600 rpm (52 mph) yet hangs on to close to 6,000 rpm (93 mph) before changing to top. This last change is fine when driving the car hard but we found that even in gentle running third gear was held for too long.

Changing gear manually improves control and overcomes the reluctance to move down from third to second. If 'S' is selected, this also overcomes the reluctance to change while also extending the kickdown availability. But any manual override may be considered by many to defeat the main object of having automatic transmission.

The lever itself moves smoothly enough and owners of previous Mercedes models will be familiar with the P-R-N-D-S-L shift lever pattern, with the zigzag gate set in such a way that accidental selection of an undesirable gear is almost impossible.

With first gear only available for moving off from standstill and top still too low for totally unfussed high-speed cruising, we cannot but feel the Mercedes has failed to take full advantage of having a four-speed transmission, and we are also disappointed that in this application it fails to match the smoothness of the 'old' three-speeder fitted to the 450.

HANDLING

★★ ★★ We have come to expect impeccable road manners from all Mercedes cars and the 380 SLC is no exception in this respect, though in some areas it is now beginning to show some signs of age.

Mercedes continues to use a recirculating ball steering system with power assistance and, as with the 450 SLC, it is nicely weighted, accurate and sensibly geared requiring 3.2 turns to move from lock to lock. But the system is not over-endowed with feel, particularly at speed on a motorway, and the steering wheel is still absurdly large in diameter, though its replacement with anything smaller would require a new instrument panel.

As before though, the SLC feels superbly balanced and remarkably wieldy for a car of this size and weight. On 205/70 VR 14 Dunlop SP Sport tyres, the car is immensely sure-footed and can be put through bends at remarkably high speeds, in an attitude of mild understeer which at the limit gives way to a slight tail-out posture. The forgiving nature of the chassis means that if you are forced to lift off in mid-corner, the rear will only mildly step out of line.

On tight, low-speed corners, coarse use of the accelerator will cause the rear of the car to slide smartly outwards, though the fitting of a limited slip differential as standard has reduced the previous car's tendency for plumes of smoke to pour off the spinning inside wheel.

Stability at speed is generally good but strong cross winds at speeds above 80 mph can cause the car to pitch and sway, requiring concentration to keep it on line.

But the car's Achilles Heel is its wet weather traction. Accelerating away from road junctions can easily cause the rear wheels to lose their grip and the tail to slide out of line, albeit an action which is quickly and easily corrected. Likewise care needs to be taken while negotiating traffic islands in the wet for as the car's attitude changes it is all too easy for the rear end to break away.

BRAKES

★★ ★ With 10.9 in ventilated discs at the front and slightly larger 11.0 in discs at the rear, the 380's dual circuit braking system excels in being able to stop one and a half tons of car from speed without fuss or drama. Not only do the brakes

MOTOR ROAD TEST NO 4/81

| ★★★★ excellent | ★★★★ good | ★★★★ average | ★★ poor | ★ bad |

Make: Mercedes-Benz
Model: 380 SLC
Maker: Daimler-Benz AG, 7000 Stuttgart 60, West Germany
UK Importers: Mercedes-Benz (UK) Ltd, Millington Road, Hayes, Middlesex. Tel: 01-573 7777
Price: £17,282.00 basic plus £1,440.17 Car Tax plus £2,808 VAT equals £21,530.50 total

inspire confidence, but they are also very smooth and progressive and perfectly weighted.

Despite these favourable subjective impressions, the system was only partially successful during our tests at MIRA. We found it almost impossible to apply a pressure of over 50 lbs to the pedal at 30 mph without the front wheels locking, and for this reason our best stop was only 0.91g with a 56 lb pedal pressure and the front brakes locking up. The norm for a car in this class is closer to 1g. Braking hard from 70 mph also resulted in the front wheels locking and again the 0.78g deceleration, from a 36 lb pedal pressure, must be seen as mediocre.

Loaded up with a substantial 1000 lbs on board, the 380 displayed no such locking-up problems in our rigorous fade test, which involves 21 successive stops from (in this case) 86 mph, at 45 sec intervals and at 0.6g, with the exception of the sixth and 21st stops which are at maximum g. Starting at 32 lbs the pedal pressure rose to 40 lbs by the third stop and varied remarkably little thereafter. Even in the last maximum g stop, the brakes were able to slow the car with a deceleration higher than that obtained with cold brakes. The brakes were also unaffected by a soaking in the water splash.

Possibly due to poor adjustment, the test car's handbrake proved inadequate in its performance. It was unable to hold the car on the downward 1-in-3 slope and when pulled hard on at 30 mph, took a yawning 211ft to bring the car to a halt, equivalent to a poor 0.14g deceleration.

ACCOMMODATION

★★
★★
While nobody is likely to buy the Mercedes in search of maximum four-seat accommodation, the SLC is much roomier than just a two-plus-two. There is a considerable amount of legroom available in the front, with generous headroom and if you set the driver's seat for someone of average height there remains *just* enough legroom for a similarly-sized passenger behind. This arrangement is ideally suited for only short journeys as the rear seat is rather hard and shapeless and headroom is only fair.

Getting in and out of the back can be somewhat awkward because of the relatively low roofline, but with the doors open, the front seat backrests will fold forward without the need to fumble for release catches: with the engine running and the doors closed, the seat backrests will lock automatically with vacuum-operated catches.

Interior stowage is fair, with a glove locker, a tray beneath the handbrake for oddments, shallow door pockets and a first aid cabinet built into the rear parcel shelf. The boot, which holds 9.9 cu ft of our Revelation suitcases, is wide and deep and easy to load.

RIDE COMFORT

★★
★★
It is usual among cars of this class to sacrifice some ride comfort in pursuance of taut and sporting handling. But in the 380 SLC, Mercedes has managed to find a good overall ride/handling compromise — not quite as good as that of the XJS but better than the Porsche 928's.

The ride itself is firm yet very comfortable. At low speed there is some choppiness over broken surfaces but most road irregularities are soaked up without being transmitted into the passenger compartment. Only the deep ridge or pothole will cause the suspension to thump harshly. At cruising pace, however, surface irregularities are smoothed out in a most satisfying way yet there is no trace of sogginess, unlike in the Jaguar which has a tendency to 'float' over undulations at speed.

AT THE WHEEL

★★
★★
All but the tallest of drivers will find plenty of legroom in the driver's seat though the position itself is dominated by the over-large steering wheels, which can make getting in and out of the car awkward because of its closeness to the cushion. Most of our testers complained that it touched the top of their legs and that the top of the wheel itself also obscured part of the fuel gauge and the important 4000-5500 rpm section of the tachometer.

The seat itself (covered in cloth though leather is optional) is firm yet comfortable, even after a 250 mile drive. Thigh and lumbar support is good but a twisty section of road will show up the lack of side support for less well-built drivers as the seats are wide. There is plenty of fore and aft movement and the backrest can be adjusted by means of a knurled knob, but raising and lowering the seats require a spanner to adjust the seat's setting on its runners. Adjustable headrestraints are standard.

Both the brake and accelerator pedals are large and well-placed though the latter is too upright, which makes long motorway journeys tiring.

Two column-mounted stalks are provided, both on the right hand side. The larger one controls the indicators/headlamp flasher/headlamp dip facilities as well as the two-speed plus intermittent wipers and washers. With so many functions, operating it can prove over-complicated especially as the stalk has to be twisted anti-clockwise (towards the driver) to operate the wipers. Also mounted on the column is the switch for the excellent cruise control. The horn is operated by depressing the steering wheel boss, while the light switch is mounted on the facia to the right of the wheel. The rest of the switchgear consists of small rocker switches positioned below the centre vents.

VISIBILITY

★★
★★
With its fairly high seating position, generous glass area (for its class) and square lines, the Mercedes is an easy car to place when manoeuvring in confined spaces. Only the hefty rear three-quarter pillars and to a lesser extent the louvred rear quarterlights, detract from the good all-round visibility. The internally adjustable (not electric) driver's and passenger door mirrors have a good field of view as too has the interior rear view mirror.

The headlamps are powerful on both dip and main beam and not only do the lamps have a wash/wipe system but they can be adjusted for height from a drum-type switch on the centre con-

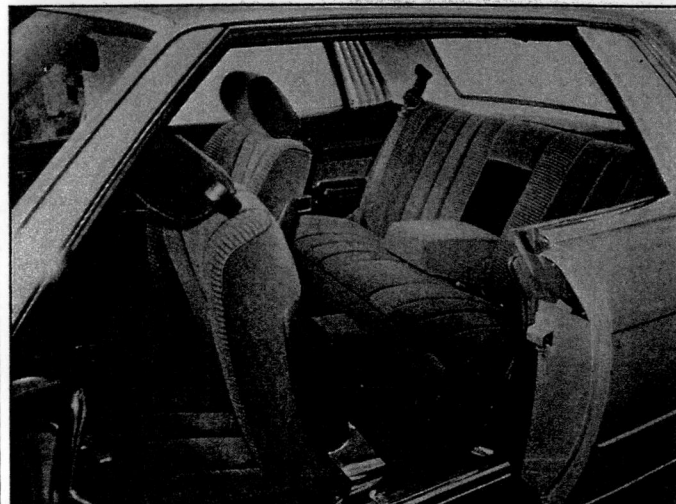

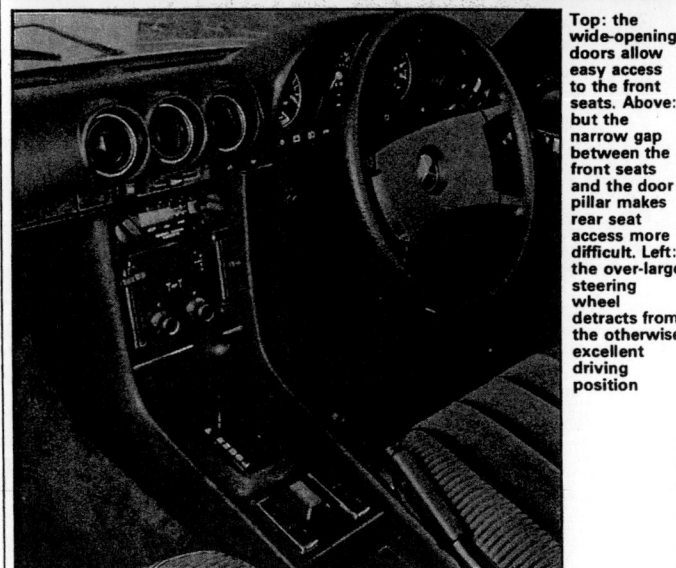

sole inside the car.

A comprehensive, if correspondingly complex, wash/wipe system provides intermittent and flick wash/wipe as well as two constant speeds. The wipers clear the screen well though they leave an arc of unwiped screen at the bottom in front of the driver.

INSTRUMENTS

★★
★★
Unlike the new 'S' class saloons, which now have their instrument cluster covered by a single pane of clear plastic, the SLC

Top: the wide-opening doors allow easy access to the front seats. Above: but the narrow gap between the front seats and the door pillar makes rear seat access more difficult. Left: the over-large steering wheel detracts from the otherwise excellent driving position

retains its three dial panel with each one covered by individual panes. Nevertheless, the instruments are clear, well-calibrated and free of reflections. The large 160 mph speedometer (5 mph optimistic at 100 mph in the test car) is flanked by a smaller tachometer with inset clock and a compound dial with a fuel gauge, oil pressure gauge, water temperature gauge and vacuum-operated econometer.

Beneath the panel is a row of six warning lights covering indicators, battery charge indicator light, main beam, brake warning and brake pad wear.

HEATING

★★
★★
Four vertical slides on the centre console control the heating and ventilation system. The slide settings are poorly marked with a series of arrows and wedges which are confusing compared with more modern layouts (the system in the new 'S' class saloon is a considerable improvement). Once mastered, and it does take some studying of the handbook, the heating system works well with air distributed to both the front and rear as well as both footwells. It is also possible for warm air to be provided to one footwell while cold air is distributed to the other.

With the four-speed blower on its highest setting, demisting is rapid and with warm air 'piped' into the doors, the side windows can also be kept clear. The fan, which is extremely quiet at all speeds, can also boost the centre cold air vents as well as the end of facia vents, these being connected to the heater.

The optional air conditioning system (an extra £1,118) can only be used to refrigerate the air and is controlled by a small knob on the centre console.

VENTILATION

★★
★★
The ventilation system is separate from the heater, and cool air enters via three centre vents mounted at face-level on the dashboard. All three are adjustable for direction but unfortunately there is only one volume control. The two end of facia vents are also adjustable for direction and are individually controlled but these are connected to the heater system.

The system works well with a strong flow of air emerging on ram effect alone, although the ventilation is fan boostable. We would have liked individual controls for the three centre outlets.

The optional air conditioning can be used to cool the air emerging from the centre vents though the output is considerably reduced and in most climates it would be an unnecessary expense.

NOISE

★★
★★
The way in which road noise is filtered out is one of the best aspects of the 380's noise suppression for tyre roar is low and so is bump-thump, apart from the occasional suspension noise on broken surfaces.

Except for under hard acceleration, the beautiful V8 is quiet and refined with only a deep hum emerging from under the long bonnet. It is not in the same league as the Jaguar in this

PERFORMANCE

CONDITIONS
Weather	Wind 10-15 mph
Temperature	47°F
Barometer	30.5 in Hg
Surface	Dry tarmacadam

MAXIMUM SPEEDS
	mph	kph
Banked Circuit	133	213
Terminal Speeds:		
at ¼ mile	88	142
at kilometre	110	177
Speed in gears (at 6300 rpm):		
1st	29	47
2nd	59	95
3rd	98	158

ACCELERATION FROM REST
mph	sec	kph	sec
0-30	3.2	0-40	2.7
0-40	4.6	0-60	4.4
0-50	6.3	0-80	6.3
0-60	8.4	0-100	9.0
0-70	11.2	0-120	12.7
0-80	14.1	0-140	16.6
0-90	17.6	0-160	20.6
0-100	23.0		
0-110	32.1		
Stand'g ¼	16.5	Stand'g km	30.0

ACCELERATION IN KICKDOWN
mph	sec	kph	sec
20-40	2.6	40-60	1.7
30-50	3.1	60-80	1.9
40-60	3.8	80-100	2.7
50-70	4.9	100-120	3.7
60-80	5.7	120-140	3.9
70-90	6.4	140-160	4.0
80-100	8.9		
90-110	14.5		

FUEL CONSUMPTION
Touring*	20.0 mpg
	14.1 litres/100 km
Overall	16.7 mpg
	16.9 litres/100 km
Govt tests	15.0 mpg (urban)
	25.7 mpg (56 mph)
	22.8 mpg (75 mph)
Fuel grade	98 octane
	4 star rating
Tank capacity	19.8 galls
	90.0 litres
Max range	390 miles
	628 km
Test distance	2131 miles
	3428 km

*Estimated consumption midway between 30 mph and maximum less 15 per cent allowance for acceleration.

BRAKES
Pedal pressure, stopping distance, and average deceleration from 30ph (48 kph).

lb	kg	ft	m	g
20	9.1	89.5	27.3	0.34
40	18.2	41.9	12.8	0.72
56	25.4	33.1	10.1	0.91
Handbrake		216	66.1	0.14

Maximum from 70 mph (113 kph)
36	16.3	211	64.4	0.78

FADE
Twenty 0.6g stops at 45 sec intervals from speed midway between 40 mph (64 kph) and maximum (86 mph, 138 kph) at gross vehicle weight.
	lb	kg
Pedal force at start	32	14
Pedal force at 10th stop	44	20
Pedal force at 20th stop	40	18

STEERING
Torque at wheel rim when parking and when cornering on 216 ft diameter circle.
	lb ft
Parking	4.0
Cornering at 0.1g	1.5
0.3g	2.5
0.6g	2.6

Turning circle between kerbs	ft	m
left	33.3	10.2
right	33.1	10.1
lock to lock	3.2 turns	
50ft diam. circle	0.8 turns	

NOISE
	dBA	Motor rating*
30 mph	63	9.5
50 mph	68	14
70 mph	74	21
Max revs in 2nd	77	26

(1st for 3-speed auto)
*A rating where 1 = 30 dBA and 100 = 96 dBA, and where double the number means double the loudness

SPEEDOMETER (mph)
Speedo	30	40	50	60	70	80	90	100
True mph	26.5	36	46	56	65	75	85	95

Distance recorder: 2 per cent fast

WEIGHT
	cwt	kg
Unladen weight*	30.7	1560
Weight as tested	34.4	1748

*with fuel for approx 50 miles

Performance tests carried out by Motor's staff at the Motor Industry Research Association proving ground, Lindley.

Test Data: World Copyright reserved; no unauthorised reproduction in whole or part.

GENERAL SPECIFICATION

ENGINE
Cylinders	V8
Capacity	3818 cc (233 cu in)
Bore/stroke	92/71.8 mm
	(3.62/2.83 in)
Cooling	Water
Block	Aluminium alloy
Head	Aluminium alloy
Valves	Ohc
Cam drive	chain
Compression	9.0:1
Fuel system	Bosch K-Jetronic mechanical fuel-injection
Bearings	5 main
Max power	218 bhp (DIN) at 5500 rpm
Max torque	224 lb ft (DIN) at 4000 rpm

TRANSMISSION
Type	4-speed automatic with torque converter

Internal ratios and mph/1000 rpm
Top	1.000:1/22.3
3rd	1.44:1/15.5
2nd	2.4:1/9.3
1st	3.68:1/6.1
Rev	5.14:1
Final drive	3.27:1

BODY/CHASSIS
Construction	Unitary all steel
Protection	Phosphating; electrophoretic dip primer

before main paint coats; pvc underbody coating; wax spray in body cavities

SUSPENSION
Front	Independent by double wishbones, coil springs, anti-roll bar.
Rear	Independent by semi-trailing arms, coil springs, anti-roll bar, 'anti-squat' geometry.

STEERING
Type	Mercedes-Benz recirculating ball
Assistance	Yes

BRAKES
Front	Ventilated disc, 10.9 in dia
Rear	Disc, 11.0 in dia
Park	On rear wheels
Servo	Yes
Circuit	Dual, split front/rear
Rear valve	No
Adjustment	Automatic

WHEELS/TYRES
Type	Steel, 6½J x 14 (alloy optional)
Tyres	Dunlop SP Sport, 205/70 VR 14

Pressures	32/36 psi F/R (normal)
	36/40 psi F/R (full load/high speed)

ELECTRICAL
Battery	12V, 66 Ah
Earth	Negative
Generator	Alternator, 980W
Fuses	20
Headlights	
type	Halogen
dip	110 W total
main	120 W total

IN SERVICE GUARANTEE
Duration ..12 months, unlimited mileage

MAINTENANCE
Free service:	at 600-900 miles
Schedule:	every 12000 miles
Int. oil change:	at 6,000 miles

DO-IT-YOURSELF
Sump:	14.1 pints, 20W/50
Gearbox:	10.9 pints, ATF Dexron
Coolant:	22.0 pints
Chassis lubrication:	none
Spark plug type	Bosch W7D, W175T30
Spark plug gap:	0.8 mm
Tappets:	hydraulic, self-adjusting

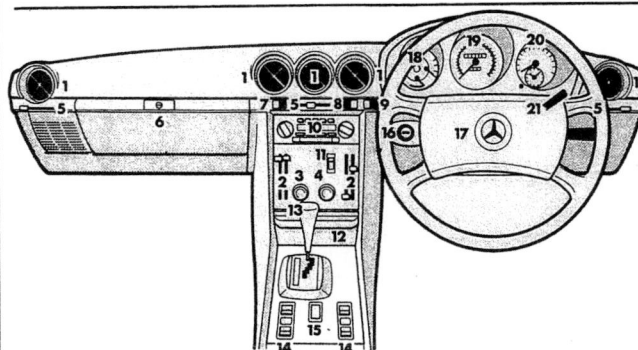

1 Fresh air vents
2 Heat and vent controls
3 Fan
4 Air conditioning (optional)
5 Vent controls
6 Locker
7 Heated rear windows
8 Electric sunroof
9 Interior light
10 Radio/cassette player
11 Headlamp height control
12 Ashtray
13 Gear selector
14 Electric windows
15 Hazard lights
16 Ignition
17 Horn
18 Fuel/watertemp/oil pressure gauge
19 Speedo
20 Tacho/clock
21 Cruise control

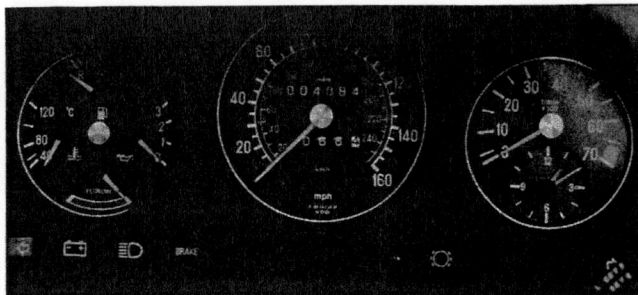

The instruments are clear, comprehensive and well-calibrated

respect but it is above the class average. Transmission whine is subdued, but by no means absent.

If there are any complaints they are concerned with the suppression of wind noise. At speeds above 60 mph noise from the wind swirling around the large door mirrors can become annoying and in very strong winds, the top of the door on the leeward side will 'pop' out of its frame accompanied by an alarming rush of wind.

EQUIPMENT

★★
★★★

A quick glance at our comparison tables shows that although the Mercedes is certainly well-equipped it is not exceptionally so and that a number of its cheaper rivals are as well as or better-equipped. Nevertheless, notable items fitted as standard to the 380 SLC include central door locking, electric windows front and rear, automatic transmission, power steering, a limited slip differential, electric sliding roof, and headlamp wash/wipe. For a car costing over £21,500 perhaps you should expect alloy wheels (£453 extra), air conditioning (£1,118) and height and tilt adjustment for the driver's seat, and a seat heater (£102). The only other extras available include self-levelling rear suspension (£332) and from February, an ABS anti-lock braking system (£830).

FINISH

★★ ★★
★★ ★★

To some, the interior of the SLC was considered rather too bland and austere for a car costing so much (especially as the test car was trimmed in black), but no one could fault the way in which it was put together either inside or out. The paintwork was extremely well done, all the panels fitted perfectly, and the doors closed with a satisfying 'clunk'.

One complaint was the almost lethargic way in which the electric windows were raised, occasionally juddering in their channels.

IN SERVICE

The 380 SLC comes with a 12 month unlimited mileage warranty. After the first free service at between 600 and 900 miles, major services are required at every 12,000 miles with a lubrication service at 6,000 miles.

A comprehensive rust-proofing process is applied to Mercedes-Benz shells at the Sindelfingen factory which includes an electrophoretic dip and a pvc underbody coating.

Under-bonnet access to the major service items is good with the dipstick, washer bottles and battery within easy reach. The spare wheel is stored flat inside the boot with the jack and tools at the side.

CONCLUSION

There are few people who will argue that the 380 SLC is one of the world's finest luxury sporting coupés: beautifully styled and superbly engineered by one of the world's most respected manufacturers. With its new all-alloy V8 engine, the car is more economical without any loss of performance and more refined than its predecessor though its new 4-speed automatic transmission is not without its shortcomings and many will consider it no match for the previous three-speed transmission. Its ride/handling compromise is certainly one of the best in its class but its handling at the limit and its poor wet weather traction are areas which need attention.

Some people might say that after close to nine years in production, Mercedes-Benz' coupé is in need of a facelift enabling it to incorporate some of the significant interior and exterior changes made to the 'S' class saloons. But until then, the 380 SLC will continue to attract a devoted following eager to own a classic thoroughbred.

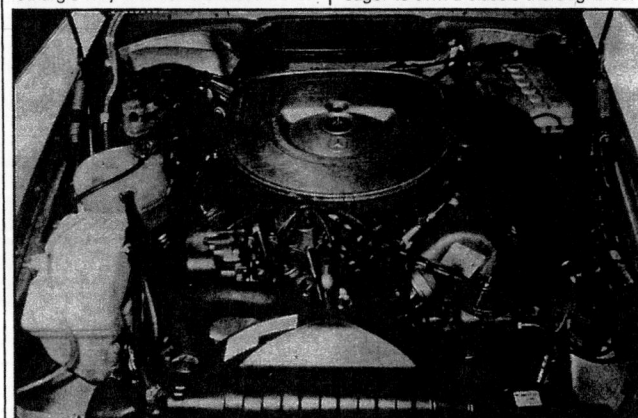

Despite the crowded engine bay, access to the major service points is good

Comparisons

PERFORMANCE	Mercedes	BMW**	Ferrari	Jaguar	Lotus**	Porsche
Max speed, mph	133.0†	138.0†	152.0†	145.0†	130.0†	140.0†
Max in 4th	—	118	123	—	116	—
3rd	98	84	91	—	83	—
2nd	59	62	65	109	60	59
1st	29	40	45	65	39	98
0-60 mph, secs	8.4	7.6	6.4	7.6	7.5	7.6
30-50 mph in 4th, secs‡	3.1	6.0	5.1	2.8	7.2	2.8
50-70 mph in top, secs‡	4.9	8.0	7.2	3.5	9.8	3.9
Weight, cwt	30.7	29.7	25.3	34.3	22.9	28.9
Turning circle, ft*	33.2	32.5	39.8	34.2	34.7	34.1
50ft circle, turns	0.8	1.0	1.3	1.1	1.15	1.05
Boot capacity, cu ft	9.9	12.5	5.0	8.4	6.6	7.3

*mean of left and right †estimated ‡kickdown for automatics **figs for manual

COSTS AND SERVICE	Mercedes	BMW	Ferrari	Jaguar	Lotus	Porsche
Price, inc VAT & tax, £	21,531	18,950	17,534	19,187	17,137	21,827
Insurance group	8	8	8	8	8	8
Overall mpg	16.7	16.5	14.1	13.5	20.6	18.5
Touring mpg	—	—	18.7	16.1	—	—
Fuel grade (stars)	4	4	4	4	4	4
Tank capacity, gals	19.8	15.4	17.2	20.0	14.7	18.9
Service interval, miles	6,000	5,000	6,000	6,000	5,000	12,000
No of dealers	97	145	18	196	30	26
Set brake pads (front) £*	18.57	22.64	19.31	31.85	19.90	52.90
Complete clutch £*	—	119.72	218.67	113.48	81.81	325.77
Complete exhaust £*	320.35	405.01	249.95	347.76	403.42	569.07
Front wing panel £*	144.56	314.39	170.66	144.90	N/A	251.88
Oil filter, £*	3.65	2.90	5.95	8.22	5.23	11.52
Starter motor, £*	101.20	120.19†	207.95	102.03	126.98†	251.23
Windscreen, £*	149.53	170.41	186.84	55.20	198.49	300.93

*inc VAT but not labour charges †Exchange

STANDARD EQUIPMENT	Mercedes	BMW	Ferrari	Jaguar	Lotus	Porsche
Adjustable steering		●		●		●
Air conditioning				●		●
Alloy wheels		●	●	●	●	●
Central door locking	●	●		●		
Cigar lighter	●	●	●	●	●	●
Clock	●	●	●	●	●	●
Cloth trim	●	●	●	†	●	●
Dipping mirror	●	●	●	●		●
Driver seat height adjust	●					
Driver seat tilt adjust		●	●			
Electric window lifters	●	●	●	●		●
Fresh air vents	●	●		●	●	●
Headlamp washers	●					●
Head restraints	●	●	●	●	●	●
Heated rear window	●	●	●	●	●	●
Intermit/flick wipe	●	●				●
Laminated screen	●	●	●	●	●	●
Locker	●	●	●	●	●	●
Passenger door mirror	●	●			●	
Petrol filler lock	●	●	●			●
Power steering	●	●		●	●·	●
Radio				●		●
Rear central armrest	●	●		●		
Rear courtesy light	●		●			●
Rear fog light	●	●	●	●	●	●
Rear wash/wipe				●		●
Remote mirror adjust	●	●		●	●	●
Rev counter	●	●	●	●	●	●
Reverse lights	●	●	●	●		●
Seat belts — rear	●	●		●		●
Seat recline	●	●	●		●	●
Sliding roof	●					
Tape player				●		●
Tinted glass	●	●	●	●	●	●
Vanity mirror	●	●	●	●	●	●

†leather

The Rivals

Other rivals to the 380 SLC include the Aston Martin V8 (£34,498), BMW 628 CSi (£16,995), Datsun 280 ZX-2 + 2 Auto (£9,936), De Tomaso Longchamps (£26,810), Lancia Gamma Coupé (£10,500), Maserati Kyalami (£30,000), Mercedes 280 SLC (£17,600), and Opel Monza 3.0 Auto (£12,939).

MERCEDES-BENZ 380 SLC — £21,531

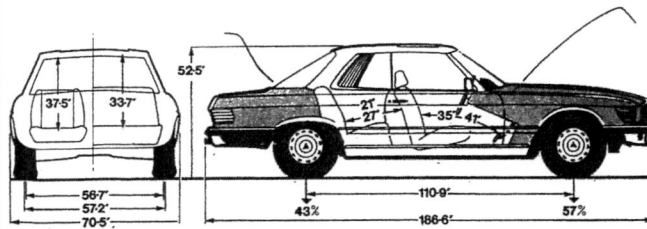

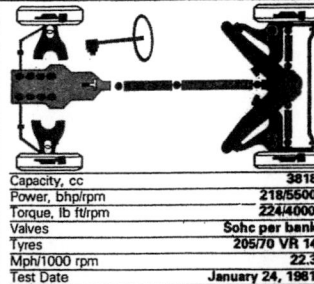

Capacity, cc	3818
Power, bhp/rpm	218/5500
Torque, lb ft/rpm	224/4000
Valves	Sohc per bank
Tyres	205/70 VR 14
Mph/1000 rpm	22.3
Test Date	January 24, 1981

New all-alloy 3.8 V8 gives Mercedes 'top-of-the range' coupé similar performance with better economy than the previous 450 SLC, though new four-speed automatic gearbox is not as refined as previous three-speeder. Excellent motorway cruiser and good ride and handling allows quick cross-country journeys. Accommodation is good for class. Comfortable and well-equipped but needs detail improvements of the new 'S' class saloons.

BMW 635 CSi AUTO — £18,950

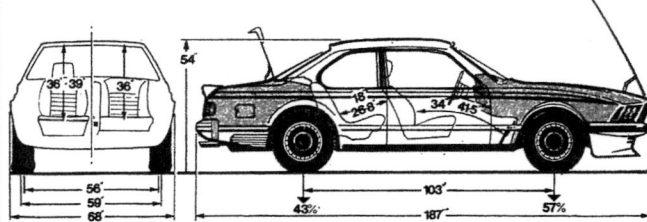

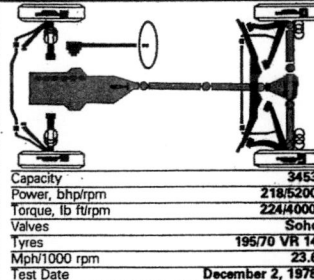

Capacity	3453
Power, bhp/rpm	218/5200
Torque, lb ft/rpm	224/4000
Valves	Sohc
Tyres	195/70 VR 14
Mph/1000 rpm	23.6
Test Date	December 2, 1978

Top-of-the-range BMW that with its large spoilers, close-ratio five-speed gearbox (as tested) and stiffened suspension is designed as very much a driver's car. Less than ideal matching of the gearing to the engine characteristics spoils what is otherwise a fine machine, for it has excellent handling, performance (for price) and reasonable economy. Rear seat is cramped and the 635 is not the quietest car of its class.

FERRARI 308 GT4 — £17,534

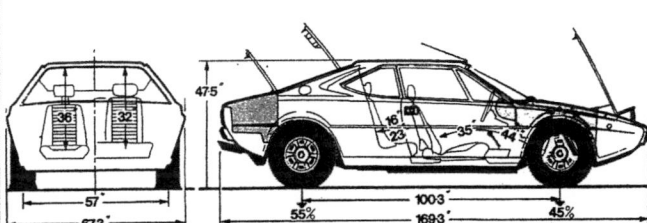

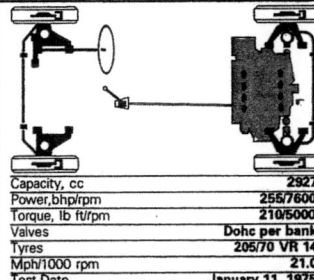

Capacity, cc	2927
Power, bhp/rpm	255/7600
Torque, lb ft/rpm	210/5000
Valves	Dohc per bank
Tyres	205/70 VR 14
Mph/1000 rpm	21.0
Test Date	January 11, 1975

Mid-engine coupé powered by 255 bhp V8 giving outstanding performance and fair economy. Mediocre gearchange. Nominally a 2+2 but tiny rear seats not suitable for adults; boot is small. Roadholding exceptional, handling less precise and responsive than that of 246 Dino. Visibility good, heating and ventilation disappointing. Although production has ceased, the replacement Mondial has just become available but will not arrive in UK till the spring.

JAGUAR XJS — £19,187

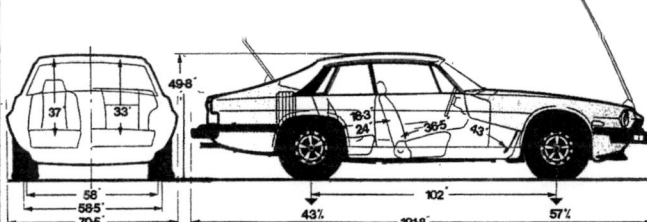

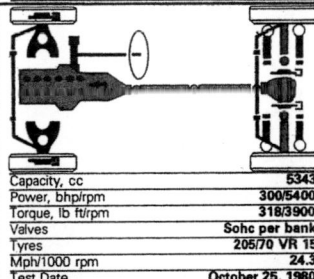

Capacity, cc	5343
Power, bhp/rpm	300/5400
Torque, lb ft/rpm	318/3900
Valves	Sohc per bank
Tyres	205/70 VR 15
Mph/1000 rpm	24.3
Test Date	October 25, 1980

Now available only in automatic form, the XJ-S continues to provide an exceptional combination of performance, refinement and comfort at a price none of its rivals can beat. Economy improved with new digital fuel-injection, though still a thirsty car. Styling hasn't improved with familiarity, and cramped in the rear, but if you can afford the fuel bills the XJ-S remains one of the world's finest and most desirable cars.

ELITE S 2.2 AUTO — £17,137

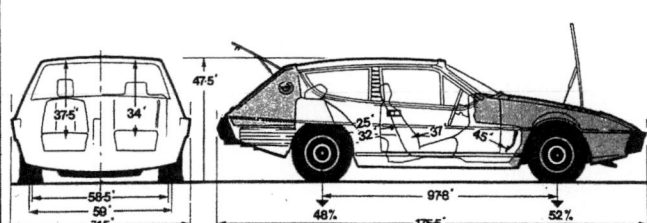

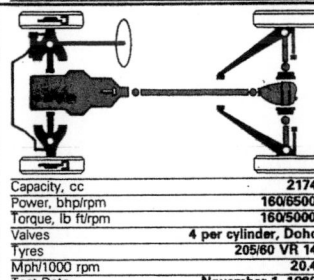

Capacity, cc	2174
Power, bhp/rpm	160/6500
Torque, lb ft/rpm	160/5000
Valves	4 per cylinder, Dohc
Tyres	205/60 VR 14
Mph/1000 rpm	20.4
Test Date	November 1, 1980

Still a trend setter for exotic cars of the future. Exceptional handling and roadholding and good performance (for manual version) and refinement despite an engine which, even with the increase in capacity, is only 2.2-litres. Economical for such a fast car with four proper seats and a useful tailgate. Very comfortable and lavishly equipped. Visibility to the rear can be a problem but apart from this the Elite is now difficult to fault.

PORSCHE 928 AUTO — £21,827

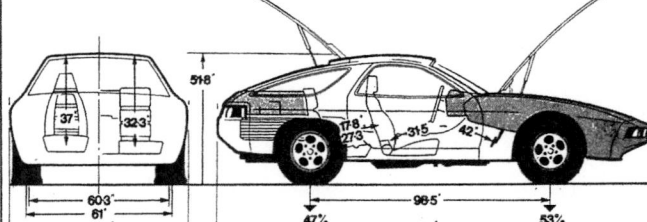

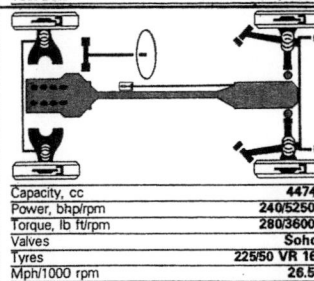

Capacity, cc	4474
Power, bhp/rpm	240/5250
Torque, lb ft/rpm	280/3600
Valves	Sohc
Tyres	225/50 VR 16
Mph/1000 rpm	26.5
Test Date	Not Published

Porsche's luxury sports car in its latest form is as quick as the Jaguar. Super-refined engine and low wind noise but potential refinement let down by excessive tyre roar. Superlative road holding, and excellent handling in all but the most extreme conditions, with mediocre ride. Excellent brakes. Beautifully made and lavishly equipped. Very spacious for two, but cramped rear seat. Economical for its class.

Mercedes-Benz
450 SLC sports coupé

Dignified, beautiful and vigorous, a R30 000
super-car shows the qualities
which justify its cost...

20 000 km test

What makes a car worth nearly R30 000? To the ordinary motorist, a car with a price tag that high is an impossible luxury. But the Mercedes 450 SL and SLC are being assembled in South Africa at the rate of about 40 units a month, with a small queue of eager buyers waiting for them — an indication that they must have merits beyond their obvious prestige value.

A YEAR-LONG TEST

To the man who owns one — usually he is a business or professional man, and a leader in his field — this graceful and distinguished sports coupé represents some of the ultimate standards in automotive engineering, manufactured to the quality levels which he demands.

Having completed an intimate assessment of the 450 SLC over a period of nearly 12 months, we are able to give a fair report on the ingredients which constitute its appeal to wealthy and discriminating motorists, based on 20 000 km of South African motoring.

EXCLUSIVE FEATURES

We fetched the SLC at the Car Distributors Assemblies' plant in East London on April 15, 1977. This was the start of a round-the-Republic journey which took us from East London to Durban, on to Johannesburg and then through Bloemfontein to Cape Town.

The car had only been on the market a short while at that time, and understandably attracted a considerable amount of attention. Remarks of sheer admiration were mixed with sarcasm, such as: "For that price, where is the second bedroom?"

But a look at the engineering and equipment specification of this quite superlative car tends to put the price into perspective. The main items that stand out prominently on first acquaintance — and many of which are exclusive features — are:

● Electrically-driven windows and sliding roof.

(Continued overleaf)

COST SUMMARY
Total distance covered . . 19 071 km
Total running costs R1 698,52
Cost per kilometre 8,9c
(These figures do not include the original purchase price or depreciation of the vehicle, but do include all actual running costs incurred over the 19 071 km test period.)

41

● Self-seeking Becker "Mexico" radio with built-in tape deck and four stereo speakers, with speaker balance control.
● Automatic aerial activated just by switching the radio on or off — and also retracted when switching the ignition off.
● Six permutations for headlights, foglights and parking lights.
● High-quality air-conditioning for both cooling and heating, which is also channeled through the doors for demisting side windows and ventilating door panels. Controls are easy to use.

FULL INSTRUMENTATION

● Velour upholstery, in a soft mushroom shade. (This was only available for a short time — leather is standard now.)
● The car is fully-instrumented, with large speedometer at centre, tachometer, clock, fuel gauge, temperature gauge and oil pressure gauge, together with warning lights for turn indicators, main beam, hand brake and other functions.
● The car is equipped with light alloy wheels which have a sporting look and improve road holding, because the aluminium alloy reduces unsprung mass. The lighter wheel follows the road surface unerringly, and ensures maximum tyre adhesion.

PRACTICAL EQUIPMENT

Other less-obvious, but important practical features of the car include:
● A central locking system, vacuum-operated from the driver's door, though individual locks can be operated separately by hand. This covers doors, trunk and petrol cap cover. The system works off the inlet manifold with a storage tank to supply pressure when the engine is not running.
● From the same system, vacuum-operated catches hold the seat backs in place when the doors are closed. These are released by opening the doors or by pressing a small vacuum release button at the rear seat.
● First-aid emergency kit and comprehensive tool kit.
● Glove box light which doubles as a removeable torch.

MECHANICAL FEATURES

The 450 SLC has several important mechanical features:
● The 4520 cm^3, dual-overhead-camshaft, V8, oversquare engine is a powerhouse producing 160 kW at 5000 r/min (in Imperial terms, 206 b-h-p!)
It has mechanically-operated fuel injection, giving instant pedal response and excellent cold-start characteristics. The warm air regulator controls the warm-up phase by enriching the fuel content — no pedal "pumping" is necessary, and in fact, the accelerator should not be touched before a cold start.
Three-speed Daimler-Benz torque-convertor automatic transmission is used — feature of which is that the car, unlike

most automatics, can be push-started. There is a handsome selector on the console, which can be used as a clutchless gearshift.

REFINED SUSPENSION

The car has diagonal swing axles at rear with anti-squat features. The semi-trailing arms, wheel carriers and torsion bar stabiliser are designed so that when the car is driven off, there is no sinking of the rear end. To counter "dive" under braking, the rear suspension is designed to pull down the rear end.

The steering column is telescopically collapsible and the power steering gives light control at low speed, without detracting from accuracy and road feel at speed.

A power-assisted, independent front and rear dual-circuit brake system is used.

Other typical Mercedes design features found throughout the range, but which were pioneered on the 350/450 SL/SLC models, include internally-ventilated disc brakes at the front to speed up cooling and reduce fade (rear discs are not internally ventilated, as they take much less load and need correspondingly less cooling capacity); and windscreen wipers located almost in the middle line of the car, allowing the blades to travel parallel with the air flow throughout their sweep.

DIRT-REPELLING LENSES

Profiled windshield pillars are designed to keep water off the side windows, and there is a rain trough over the rear window to keep it clear. Ribbed rear light lenses remain clear to maintain lighting power, even in very muddy or dusty conditions.

There is an effective, internally-adjustable driver's door mirror, "aggressively-shaped," which folds back for safety reasons — but a similar mirror should also be fitted to the passenger side, we feel.

OUTSTANDING ROADHOLDING

The car's structure incorporates safety features such as re-inforced roof frame and pillars for roll-over safety, progressive front and rear end deformation, counter-balanced door locks to keep doors closed under strong side forces, doors designed to resist side impacts, fuel tank filler pipe designed to bend rather than split, and smooth-surfaced, energy-absorbing instrument panel.

These are the "designed-in" features of the car. Add to this a handsome and distinctive shape, and one can appreciate the admiration that this car has attracted in the 6 years that it has been on world markets.

The aerodynamic nose and headlight design, coupled with the heavy rubber strips in the bumpers and the rubber beading down the side of the car give the 450 the image that its performance deserves. Even the upright three-pointed star is replaced by a badge on the front end of the bonnet, to keep the smooth line!

It is also a relatively low and sleek body line with a widely-spaced track of

1 400 mm. This gives the car outstanding roadholding, as we found throughout the test — it can be thrown through bends at extremely high speeds without any suggestion of distress.

POWERFUL SAFETY

In fact, performance is the outstanding feature of this car. Before United Car and Diesel Distributors (UCDD — general agents for Daimler-Benz in South Africa) undertook assembly of the SL and SLC in the Republic, the marque might well have had an image of a sedate, senior executive's run-about. But we were able to dispel this illusion at once.

As we proved in the inaugural test of the 450 SLC in the April 1977 issue of CAR, 100 km/h comes up in 11,9 seconds and maximum speed is a sizzling 210 km/h.

However, the real advantages under modern motoring conditions are the tremendous torque and thrust that the V8, 4,5 litre engine delivers. In about-town traffic and on freeways, overtaking is smooth, quick and safe as power is applied. In a flash, the 450 completes the manoeuvre.

SILENT CRUISING ABILITY

Add to this the interior comfort and the "climate control" features of the sophisticated air-conditioning and ventilation system, and you have (in contrast to the performance) one of the most noise-free cruising cars we have ever driven. As we reported in the original Road Test, the engine is magnificently insulated and runs quietly under the influence of long-legged gearing, while a large-capacity tailpipe muffler eliminates exhaust noise and the sealed ventilation system prevents wind roar.

One item which did disappoint us was the noise level from the tyres when cruising on smooth freeways. Dunlop SP 93 205/70-VR-14 steel-belted radials are fitted, and we found that they created a whine on smooth surfaces which was a real intrusion on the stillness of the interior, even with the windows closed. It is a design feature which we have picked up on a number of our test cars, and which needs looking at by motor companies and tyre companies alike.

SEATING COMFORT

Inside the car, one sits fairly low — a disadvantage for short-statured drivers and passengers, because on our test unit the windscreen wipers did not lie flush with the windscreen edge, on account of their length. The bonnet also takes on a higher line than is apparent from outside the car, but this is something that one soon gets used to.

In fact, first impressions from the driver's seat are of a heavy, almost cumbersome, car — but these are soon dispelled by the performance and comfort, and the 450 gives the feeling of fitting like a well-designed shoe!

The 450 seats four people comfortably, once the rear passengers have got in. Access to the rear is only just satis-

IMPERIAL DATA

Imperial-measure equivalents for basic operating data and costs are given below for comparative purposes and for the benefit of readers in non-metric countries:

Test distance . . . . 11 852 miles
Petrol consumed . . . . 637,1 gallons
Oil consumed . . . . nil
Average road economy . . 18,6 m-p-g

factory, and certainly not easy for older passengers. But then the car is designed as a 2-door sports coupé, and the room for two (or maybe three) at the rear is a bonus when viewed in this light.

BIG, SOLID DOORS

A feature which caused comment throughout the test period was the heaviness of the doors, which women passengers found difficult to open or close.

While this is a negative feature, it also reflects the extremely solid construction of the car — and we noticed how a number of components such as door stays and suspension arms are extremely ruggedly built and strengthened.

Driving controls reflect the car's image of being a real man's car. From pistol grip gear change to four-spoke rugged steering wheel, large door mirror and low-slung road stance, this car transmits the feeling of "let's go!"

And when you go, you go well and smoothly, aided by one of the best speed control units that we have tried — the VDO Tempomat with simple and precise stalk control on the steering column. The lever operates in 4 directions to allow full range adjustment: speed up or down, disengage and re-engage. The only other stalk on the steering column gives headlight flash, windscreen wash and windscreen wiper 3-speed control.

SMOOTH AUTOMATIC SHIFT

In service and on the open road the 450 SLC offered superb comfort and driving satisfaction. The firmly-shaped seats, in typical Mercedes fashion, make long-distance driving a pleasure, while the automatic trnasmission was particularly outstanding and we could sometimes hardly detect its progress through the gears. It is a completely-smooth operation from start to maximum speed, at normal throttle opening.

About town and in manoeuvring for parking, the power steering, readily available engine torque and turning circle of 11,5 metres made for easy driveability. The 450 SLC is bigger than it looks, with overall length of 4,750 metres compared to the Mercedes 123 models at 4,725 metres, and the S-class models at 4,960 metres.

The car gave exemplary service, with only one or two minor problems.

SHOCK ABSORBERS FAILED

At just over 2000 km, the alternator belt broke, possibly due to over-tightening at the plant, and this was replaced by

Cargo Motors in Illovo, Johannesburg.

Then at the 15 000 km service, carried out at Stanley Porter's, Cape Town, the left front tyre was showing excessive wear, probably due to incorrect wheel alignment, so both rear tyres were moved to the front and the spare and the right front were moved to the rear wheels.

At the same service, we reported a noisy suspension at the rear, and Stanley Porter's, Cape Town, found that the original Bilstein shock absorbers needed replacing. Fichtel and Sachs shock absorbers were fitted, but after the 20 000 km test programme was completed, the trouble recurred, and was traced to a fault in a radius-arm rubber mounting. It was attended to under warranty, and we had no further trouble.

EFFICIENT SERVICING

Servicing throughout the test period was carried out efficiently and correctly, as befits a car of this price. At the first service (carried out at Natal Motor Industries in Durban) the wheel alignment was checked and set.

The second service was at Stanley Porter's in Cape Town; and an intermediate lubrication and oil change was carried out at 13 600 km, at the recommendation of Stanely Porter's.

REASONABLE RUNNING COSTS

The third service was again at Stanley Porter's, Cape Town, when — in addition to the maintenance service — the brakes were bled and the battery "neutralised" and acid pads fitted, both items at an extra charge. In addition, the tyres were changed and shock absorbers attended to (as mentioned), driver's door alignment was adjusted and window mechanism lubricated, as was the automatic aerial which was not retracting fully.

For those who can afford a car at this price, running costs are likely to be incidental. Servicing costs were certainly not unduly high, and this should apply throughout much of the life of the car.

Overall fuel consumption, by conventional standards, was high at 15,2 litres/100 km, but not excessive for an engine of this size and right in line with the German factory figure of 14,5 litres/100 km at 110 km/h. Our "best" of 12,9 litres/100 km would give a range of nearly 700 km on a country trip.

This was, in fact, achieved on a run from Beaufort West to Johannesburg, and it also should be added that this was with full-blooded driving, as high as the current speed limit allows.

SUMMARY

One running cost item which was so high that it even caused amusement was comprehensive insurance, for which the best quote we obtained was R700 per year — one company asked for an excess of R3000 on all claims!

The built-in qualities of the 450 SL/SLC models, coupled with their high degree of exclusivity (only a limited number are being made available in South

INITIAL COSTS

Original price R28 475,00
Licensing:—
    Registration fee R10,00
    1977 licence R48,00
    Number plates. R12,00
    Total R70,00
Insurance (12 months):—
    Third Party R22,60
    Comprehensive R700
    Total R722,60
(The comprehensive insurance figure was based on a quote for a driver over 25 years with full no claim bonus using the car for private and business use.)

RUNNING COSTS

Petrol:—
    2 898,9 litres R777,57
Oil . . . . nil
    Total R777,57

SERVICING AND REPAIRS

(Including parts and labour)
1 093 km:
    1 000 km service (1st inspection)
    D I Service . . . . .No charge
    Check and set W/H . . . . .No charge
    Oil and parts. . . R10,66 (Oil R8,00)
7 779 km:
    7 500 km service (2nd Inspection) No charge
    Oil and parts. . R19,29 (Oil R12,81)
13 628 km:
    Extra oil change. R11,40 (Oil R8,48)
15 667 km:
    15 000 Maintenance Service . . 44,20
    Bleed Brake system 5,00
    Neutralize battery and fit
    acid pads 2,00
    Clean engine . . . . N/C
    Spares as per req 11,44
    Oils 15,96
    Workshop materials, acid pads,
    paraffin, brake fluid, copper slip
    and Bosch grease 8,40
    Total 87,00

TOTAL COSTS

Licensing
(12 months pro rata) R70,00
Insurance
(12 months pro rata) R722,60
Petrol. R777,57
Servicing and Repairs. . . . R128,35
Total R1 698,52

PERFORMANCE

Fuel consumption:
    Overall fuel consumption 15,2 litres/
                                      100 km
    Best achieved (open road) 12,9
    litres/100 km (Long distance
    Beaufort West to Johannesburg)
    Overall oil consumption . . . . . . nil
Tyre life:
    Make of tyre. . . Dunlop SP 93 Steel
                                     Radials
    Size of tyre . . . . . . 205/70 V R14
    Tread wear pattern . . . . . (see text).
    (The tyres were rotated during this test front to back.)

Africa, we are told) will make them a real collector's item.

The car's qualities of superb comfort and convenience, coupled with magnificent performance, are a contrast found in very few cars — and for those lucky few who have the cash to indulge in motoring pleasure at this price, they get a car which is the experience of a lifetime to own! ∎

The R107 roadster enjoyed the longest production run of any Mercedes–Benz model. John Olson offers buyers some essential insight into the evolution of this ever–present SL.

Height of
popularity

Mercedes-Benz built around a quarter of a million R107 SLs and introduced eight engine options over a 20-year period.

Dan Trent

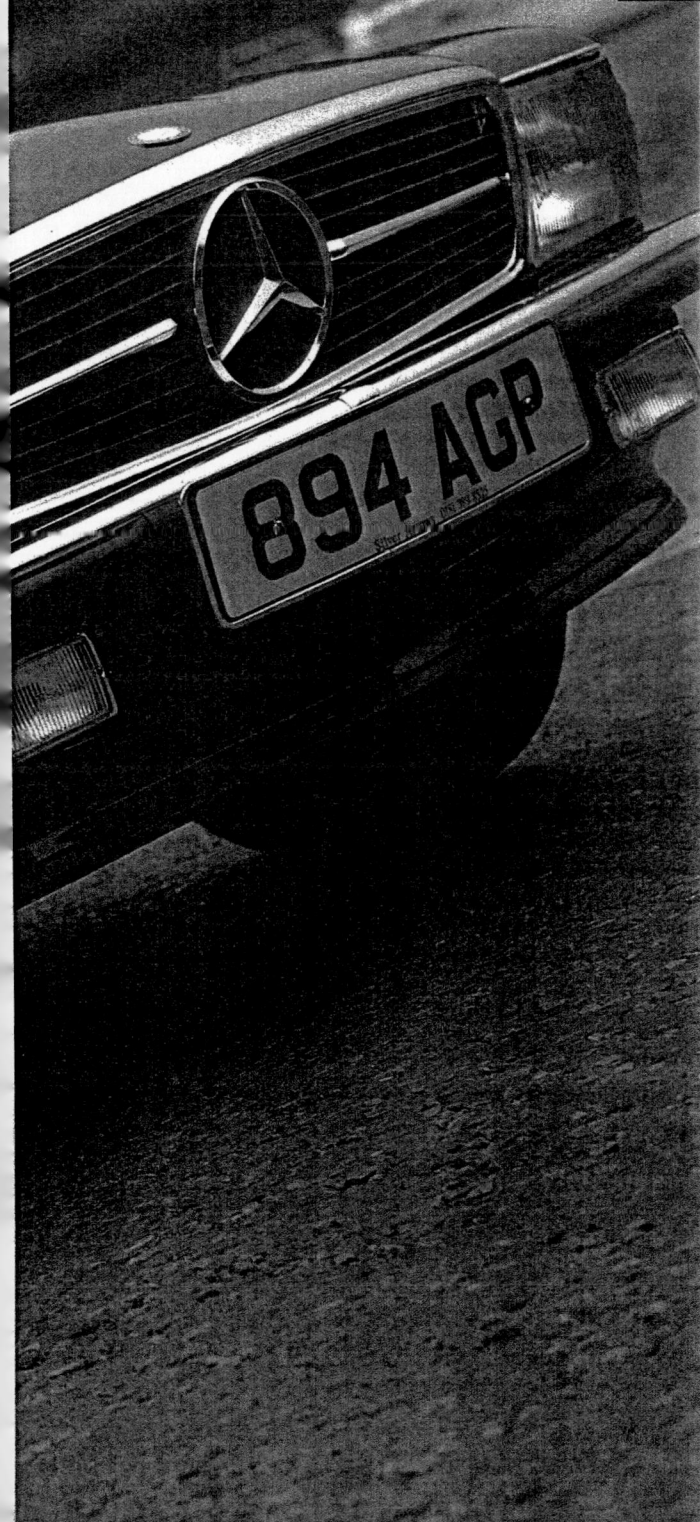

Since this is a Buyer's Guide, we'll assume that you are already attracted to this SL model. You're certainly not alone as this basic body was so popular that Mercedes-Benz found steady buyers for 19 years. Remarkably, the best-selling year was 1986, some 16 years into production! The chart below condenses many '107' facts into one quick reference. R107 is the Mercedes-Benz designation for all SL roadsters from 1971 through to 1989 plus the SLC (the five-passenger coupés built between 1971 and 1981).

When inspecting individual cars, pay attention to their chassis numbers. It is not beneath some sellers to change badges and claim a 380SL to be a 500SL, or a 500SL to be a 560SL, etc. The second cluster of three numbers in each chassis number or Vehicle Identification Number (VIN) indicates the engine type originally built (with the exception of the 560SL). The first six numbers of the engine are also given, but they are harder to find.

Outside Germany, as many as 25 percent of these SLs are titled for the first time in the year after they were built. This is not uncommon due to normal shipping and marketing time. Since condition has greater impact on values than the year in which the car was built, correcting this information probably won't alter a car's value, but it's nice to know what you're really buying. The last five numbers in a chassis or vehicle identification number (VIN) for each engine type are consecutive through all its years of production.

TRIALS AND TRIBULATIONS

Over the 19-year period of R107 production, many serious changes affected automotive markets around the world. Trouble occurred even before the first R107 was delivered when the USA announced profound new safety regulations concerning both passengers and pollution. That changes were phased in over a ten-year period was little consolation. The new crash testing standards devastated the future of such memorable cars as the MG Midget, Citroen DS and SM, the Mini Cooper, BMW CS series, Datsun 240Z, Jaguar E-Type, and the Mercedes 280SL. Fortunately for Stuttgart, the 1960s SL had already enjoyed a good production life and the next series arrived at the perfect time.

Engine plans, however, did not run as smoothly. When the 350SL reached showrooms, customers and dealers in certain other nations cried that high ⤳

FACTS AND FIGURES THE MOST IMPORTANT R107 NUMBERS

Engine Size	VIN Prefix	Engine Prefix	Model Designation	Years Built	Production Total
2.8-litre Six	107-042-	110.982	280SL	1974-1985	25,436
3.0-litre Six	107-041-	103.982	300SL	1985-1989	13,742
3.5-litre V8	107-043-	116.982	350SL	1970-1979	15,304
4.5-litre V8	107-044-	117.982 & 5	450SL	1972-1980	66,298
3.8-litre V8	107-045-	116.960 & 2	380SL	1980-1985	53,200
5.0-litre V8	107-046-	117.960 & 2 & 4	500SL	1980-1989	11,812
4.2-litre V8	107-047-	116.964	420SL	1985-1989	2,148
5.6-litre V8	A48-	117.967	560SL	1985-1989	49,347

UNDER THE SKIN KEY INSPECTION AREAS FOR POTENTIAL BUYERS

Noted for its unprecented weight and structural rigidity, the R107 design was gradually improved over two decades. Naturally, it is the early cars which are more likely to require serious attention.

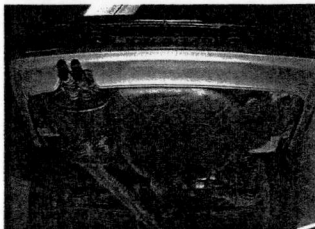

Rear valance often rusts but real horrors can lurk deeper under the skin.

Cosmetic rust around arches is common but check inner wings and subframes.

⊂ taxes for cars over 3.0 litres meant few repeat orders from 230/250/280SL owners. A severe shift in exchange rates during the 1970s caused the 450SL's suggested retail price to triple between 1971 and 1981. Then came 'grey market' turmoil which still troubles the US market today. But through it all, the amazing R107 kept selling, at five times its original price by its final year.

When the R107 SL was only a twinkle in Rudolf Uhlenhaut's eye, one thing was certain – the new roadster would be powered by a V8. Indeed, Daimler-Benz was woefully slow offering V8s. Detroit's luxury marques all had more than a decade of successful V8 production when M-B's sole V8 arrived in the 1964 Grand Mercedes 600 (at twice the price of a Cadillac Fleetwood).

The 3.5-litre V8 that finally debuted at the 1969 Frankfurt Auto Show was (and still is) an efficient design of 200bhp that only weighed 55lb more than the 2.8-litre straight-six it replaced. Until the United States' Environmental Protection Agency (EPA) announced a whole decade of progressively stricter pollution restrictions, Stuttgart thought the 3.5 V8 would be the ideal size for many years. Studying the new regulations, it was decided the best way to retain the new SL's performance was moving power and torque to lower engine speeds. That was best accomplished with larger cylinders, i.e. the 4.5-litre motor. Not needing the extra engine size in Europe confronted M-B with a marketing dilemma. Should it offer two engines in Europe? Could it offer a

450SL only in the USA without upsetting other markets? Could it do the latter by calling the 4.5-litre V8 a 350SL worldwide, regardless of which engine was installed? Each choice posed problems. Stuttgart chose the latter.

When the first cars arrived in American showrooms in late 1971 (the 1972 model year) dealers dutifully informed shoppers that even though the label on the boot said 350SL, it really had a 4.5-litre engine. Prospects rolled their eyes with obvious suspicion. Why would Stuttgart do a thing like that? Dealers quickly tired of explaining and let factory representatives have an earful. In the autumn of 1972, as 1973 models were introduced, a personal letter went out to all USA 350SL purchasers from the

President of Mercedes-Benz North America affirming that their cars had 4.5-litre engines. The letter announced that effective with the 1973 model year, all 4.5-litre cars would be labelled 450SL. Further, if the owners wished, they would receive a 450SL badge to replace the 350SL label on the boot lid of their cars. It is unknown how many owners accepted this offer. Both remain in the market place. Typical performance differences can only be detected in the best tuned cars.

THE TWIN-CAM 280SL

Initial sales of the R107 SL were gratifying – as is always the case a long backlog of buyers poured in for the first V8 SL. During the first three years (1971-1973), sales exceeded five years of 280SL sales. M-B could

Door bottoms, sills and suspension mounting points are common rust spots.

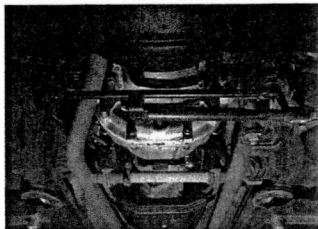

Engines and gearboxes are sturdy if well maintained; exhausts can be pricey.

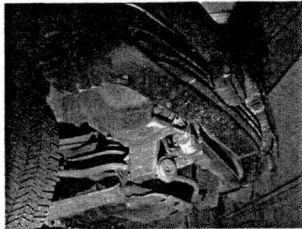

Jacking on sump can cause serious damage; also check engine mounts.

OWNER'S VIEW

Freddie Price's award-winning 300SL is a constant pleasure.

have sold even more if it had been willing to retain a six-cylinder engine, as many countries impose heavy taxes on engines over 3.0 litres. To meet the USA's 1970s crash test standards, the R107 had gained 350lb over its predecessor. Despite this weight, the new V8 delivered almost the same MPG as the six while raising top speed by 10mph and reducing 0-60mph acceleration by two seconds.

However Mercedes was at work on a new twin-cam six that first appeared in the 'new generation' 250 sedans and coupé in 1971 (the M110 engine with 166lb/ft of torque at 4,000rpm). It was lighter than the M130 unit but torque and bhp figures didn't improve. The call for a six did not subside and was magnified by the end of the orders backlog

and a slight recession in 1974 which led to an alarming drop in SL sales. Finally, for the 1975 model year (commencing in August 1974), the twin-cam six was added to the line along with a five-speed manual transmission option. It never became a huge seller but these models have accrued a loyal owner group that prefers the simplicity of a six.

In 1974, '5 mph' bumpers were added to USA-equipped cars and a catalytic converter followed in 1975. K-Jetronic (CIS) fuel injection was introduced in 1976. It is considered easier to tune. 1977 brought wood veneer to the radio, A/C and heater controls between the seats, while ABS brakes became an option in Europe during 1979 and finally made it to the States in 1985.

Some six-cylinder fans regard the

1986-1989 300SL to be the ultimate R107. Introduced at the same time as the 420SL and 560SL, they all enjoy an entirely redesigned front suspension in response to changing tyre technology. Larger (284mm) front brakes and 15-inch wheels also became standard. CIS-E fuel injection and an EZL (computer-controlled crankshaft firing) ignition system were also introduced in 1986.

COMPETITION BACKGROUND

The 1970s found M-B serving two masters: the new-found wealth of the Middle East (including the nation of Kuwait owning 13 percent of Daimler-Benz stock) while much of the world was hunkering down for a shortage of oil. Mercedes-Benz found itself building the 69

A pristine example of a late model SL, Freddie Price's 1986 300SL has won numerous awards at club events and continues to delight its enthusiastic owner. Having started his classic Mercedes owning days with a 1971 350SL Freddie has come full circle by returning to the R107 model and he's in no doubt as to the attraction.

"The styling is dateless with nice amounts of chrome," he says, "plus you get a 'modern' six-cylinder, unleaded engine." Over the three years he's owned it, work has been minimal, comprising a new propshaft coupling, middle box and hood cover lid, and Freddie seems sold on the late models' modern improvements. As he says: "These cars are good on a normal day but on a sunny day they're fantastic!"

"THE TWIN-CAM SIX NEVER BECAME A HUGE SELLER BUT THESE MODELS HAVE ACCRUED A LOYAL OWNER GROUP THAT PREFERS THE SIMPLICITY OF A SIX"

super saloon concurrent with detuned economy cars and diesels. The performance orientation was served by increasingly open involvement in long-distance rallies. Favourite bodies became the Type 123, a mid-sized sedan, and the SLC, basically an R107 SL stretched by fourteen inches behind the driver.

Three Mercedes 450SLCs were entered in the 30,000km South American Rally in 1978. All three finished with Andrew Cowan and Colin Milkin winning. Even before that victory, the search for the next winning technology coincided nicely with development of M-B's light-weight, alloy engine block without metal cylinder liners. FIA requirement for the rallies entered by Mercedes was that a minimum of 500 cars be sold to the public. This gave the edge to the SLC to receive the first alloy V8s. The 450 SLC 5.0 debuted at the 1977 Frankfurt Auto Show. Sometimes called Mercedes' answer to the Porsche 928, the 5.0 weighed in at slightly less than the much-shorter 450SL. It would be over a year later before the car's first rally which resulted in a sensational win in the 5,600km Bandama Rally.

In fact, the SLC captured the first four places. An increased rally schedule was planned for 1980, at last including SLs, four 320bhp alloy V8s campaigned by Scuderia Kassel.

Public sales of 500SLs began in April 1980 with 501 built that year, not coincidentally the number required by the FIA. It should be noted that these earliest production 5.0-litre engines (those sold to the public) were detuned slightly to 240bhp, but this was still higher than the output of the 231bhp engine used from October 1981 through to July 1989. Mercedes also introduced the new four-speed automatic transmission in April 1980.

PERFORMANCE COMPROMISE

Between air pollution and the oil prices, 1970s automotive engineers had their hands full; retain some semblance of performance, clean up emissions and raise MPG. The diesel engine has always been a big part of the Mercedes-Benz response (up to 50 percent of total production in some years) but never for the SL. For Europe, a 3.8-litre V8 version of the new alloy engine was developed concurrent with the 5.0-

litre, also superseding the iron block 4.5 in 1980. In Europe, the 3.8's torque and power were down, but the engine came impressively close to matching the 450SL's top speed and sprint time, with improved economy.

For the USA, another nightmare emerged. EPA's latest concoction was 'CAFE', a synonym for Corporate Average Fuel Economy, a fleet-wide average MPG any company selling in the USA had to achieve to avoid annual per-car fines multiplying into millions of dollars. Some companies such as Jaguar paid dearly, while Mercedes-Benz responded by shipping more diesel models including the popular 300CD, the first diesel coupé the USA had seen. For USA-bound SLs (and SEL and SEC models) Stuttgart detuned the new 3.8-litre alloy V8 from 218bhp to 155 (less than the six-cylinder engine) and gave it a single row, steel timing chain. Considering that many companies including Ferrari had begun using rubber timing belts, M-B's choice wasn't exotic. This became the only V8 available in the USA from 1981 ⊃

OWNER'S VIEW

Tony Gray took on a tired 350SL and returned it to glory.

Deliberately taking on a 107 in poor condition can be a recipe for disaster but Tony Wade had no qualms when he bought his 1972 350SL five years ago. "It was a bit of a heap when I bought it," he admits, "but I intended to invest time and money in it and that's what I did; it's had a lot of money spent on it over the years but it was exactly the right model and colour so I just had to have it." Following a thorough restoration a restless Tony has actually put the car on the market but that doesn't mean he's lost any feeling for the model. "If I could hang it up on the wall I would," he jokes. "It's 30 years-old but it compares well with anything modern although it only comes out on sunny weekends."

Far left: Lusty 5.0-litre alloy V8 was first introduced in 1980.

Left: Graceful 107 lines are still eye-catching after 30 years.

Below: Functional, comfortable cabin is spacious and extremely durable.

> "IN EUROPE, THE 3.8'S TORQUE AND POWER WERE DOWN, BUT THE ENGINE CAME IMPRESSIVELY CLOSE TO MATCHING THE 450SL'S TOP SPEED AND SPRINT TIME, WITH IMPROVED ECONOMY"

to 1985 and CAFE penalties were avoided until 1984, but several disasters arose nonetheless. Those single timing chains were breaking prematurely just after the 48,000-mile warranty period.

In fairness, many original owners were converted to dual chains under warranty extensions and second owners with out-of-warranty cars were supplied with free parts. Were M-B engineers thrown off by a misconception that Americans might actually obey their 55mph speed limits? Chains that didn't break stretched to the point that tuning was mediocre on already underpowered engines – timing chains directly affect acceleration and MPG.

US dealers struggled to keep their customers happy for three years until dual sprockets and chains returned in 1984. A few years later, single chains were dropped from M-B replacement parts entirely and dealers were ordered to convert all future problem cars to the double row chains.

BIG-CAPACITY DEMAND

380 timing chain problems were promptly followed by the first big 'grey market' frenzy. During the early 1980s, after ten years of European exchange rate catch-up, the pendulum swung back to a high of DM3.45 to 1 US Dollar by February 1985. Americans flocking to Europe included plenty of Mercedes-Benz owners. They saw and sometimes drove 500SL models. Upon returning to the States, they visited local M-B dealers with big smiles on their faces to announce they wanted to buy a car just like the one they had enjoyed in Europe. If they said it was a 500SL, dealers explained that in the USA that car was called the 380SL. While 380SL sales were healthy during 1981-1985, many shoppers were determined to get the 5.0-litre model with its 40 percent increase in horsepower. Of course European dealers were happy to oblige and the grey market was born.

EPA/DOT converting centres popped up at every US seaport.

At first it wasn't too noticeable, but the numbers literally mushroomed. In 1983, under 10,000 privately imported cars arrived; in 1984: 25,000; 1985: 80,000. The American Mercedes-Benz Dealer Council formally accused Daimler-Benz's Board of Directors of creating a dual marketing organisation that was undermining the value of their dealerships. Try as they did, Mercedes-Benz Stuttgart could not legally place restrictions on their dealers. Indeed, in recent years DaimlerChrysler has been fined by Common Market regulations for penalising dealers who sold cars across national boundaries. The problem remains today, only the names of the countries have changed.

One clever strategy specifically targeted at curtailing offending European dealers was the introduction of the 560SL to the USA only. While actual performance differences between the European 500SL and the 560SL are indiscernible, Mercedes clientele insisted on ⮑

OWNER'S VIEW
Jeremy Watts couldn't wait to replace his superb 500SL

Performance and practicality were the two attributes which won over Jeremy Watts when he bought a low-mileage 1986 500SL six years ago. "I found the car a delight to drive and it was just so easy to live with – brilliantly built and utterly reliable during my three years of ownership."

However, there was one aspect of the car that Jeremy was less comfortable with – the styling. "A lot of people commented on what a great-looking car my SL was, but the styling proved too soft for my liking. The longer I owned it, the more attracted I became to the later R129 model and I decided to upgrade to a 300SL-24 as soon as I could afford it."

After three years and 20,000 trouble-free miles, Jeremy sold the 500SL to a close friend (who bought it for his wife).

"I'm now very happy with the R129 but I do miss the older car's V8 performance," concludes Jeremy. "I also get less attention driving my later SL, but I'm certainly not bothered about that!"

Still one of the most distinctive noses on the road.

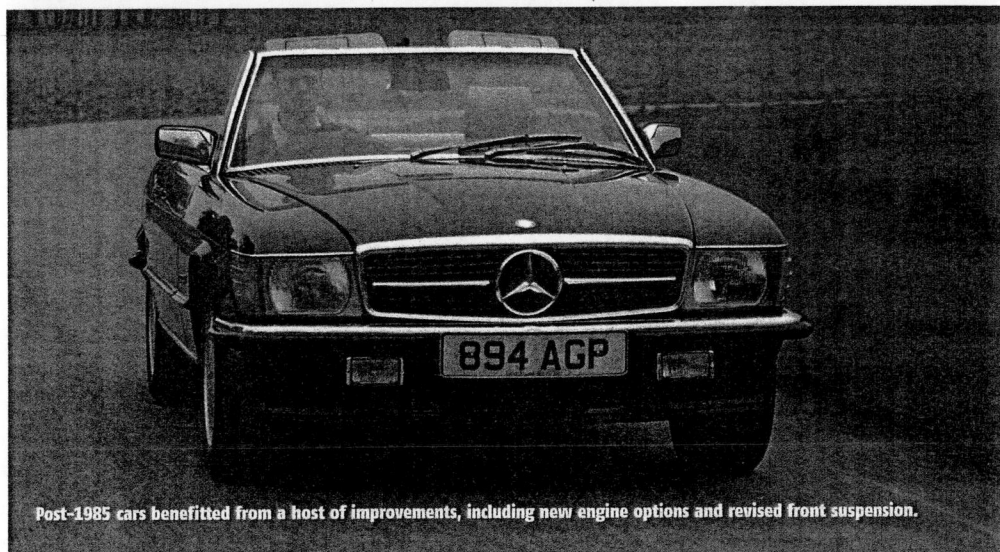

Post-1985 cars benefitted from a host of improvements, including new engine options and revised front suspension.

"NOT ONLY DID 1986 BECOME THE BEST-SELLING YEAR FOR THE R107 SL, THE 560SL SOLD BETTER THAN ALL OTHER ENGINE VARIANTS COMBINED FOR THE FINAL FOUR YEARS"

the top-of-the-line model which ensured that American dealers were back in the picture. The result: not only did 1986 become the best-selling year for the R107 SL, the 560SL sold better than all other engine variants combined for the final four years through to 1989 and a reverse grey market developed with Europeans coming to the USA to buy the 560SLs!

GUIDELINES FOR BUYERS

If money is no object, a low-mileage, original-paint 500SL or 560SL from the last production years will be most coveted by collectors decades into the future. The trouble with such stellar cars is that driving them will consume important parts of their appeal: low miles and original condition... the two things the best restoration specialists can't duplicate. Truth is, a 30,000 or even 60,000-mile Mercedes is likely to be just as reliable as one for double the money with 6,000 miles. If you know you will use the car, at least in summer, condition is more important than the year or even a particular engine. The same applies to colour; if you set your heart on a burgundy car, you will probably

pass up three nicer cars while hunting for that one elusive colour. That could happen with engines, too, so stay a little flexible. You'll find things wrong with every car you test – even the high-priced ones can be expected to need some work during your first year of ownership. As with any older car, be sure to drive it more than merely around the block – 20 minutes including motorway driving is a minimum. You'll find a surprising difference among cars of the same year simply because they're getting old. One will be tight with minimal rattles while another will feel loose in the steering or have curious drive train noises. Never assume they'll all be similar.

One of the appeals of the 280SL, 300SL and 350SL from these R107 years is availability of four- and five-speed manual transmissions. By the end of the 1960s, Mercedes-Benz customers were favouring automatic transmissions, especially on senior models including the 280SL. Manual shift enthusiasts were provided with two excellent manual boxes built by Getrag. Remember that M-B's automatic commencing with the R107 was a three-speed box, satisfactory for a V8 but less so

with the six. Today, 280SLs and 300SLs with manual five-speeds and the 350SL four-speed manual cars can be found with a little hunting. The 450, 500 and 560SL were never offered by Mercedes-Benz with manual shifting.

Lastly, a few words about safety and parts availability. For being 20 to 30 years-old, these SLs are undoubtedly the safest roadsters on the planet. In a bad accident, many would pick an R107 SL before a new econobox that costs more. And parts will be available for these SLs forever, as they were built seemingly forever! There is a strong 'support network' building worldwide plus the interchangeability of some parts from saloons. These cars have touched many lives with good memories, which spells Nostalgia with a capital N for years to come.

"YOU'LL FIND THINGS WRONG WITH EVERY CAR YOU TEST – EVEN THE HIGH-PRICED ONES CAN BE EXPECTED TO NEED SOME WORK DURING YOUR FIRST YEAR OF OWNERSHIP"

⊃ Special thanks to **Silver Arrows Automobiles TEL** 020 8789 8525, **Peter Jarvis TEL** 01322 669 081

THE MARKET WHAT'S AVAILABLE AT WHAT PRICE?

The following are random examples of R107 models recently advertised for sale in the UK.

450SL 1974 v. good cond, 4 onrs, £6,000	280SL 1985 FMBSH, gen 10,000m, £21,000
350SL 1974 man, 68,000 miles, £8,500	380SL 1985 part hist., 97,000m, £9,750
350SL 1977 H/S tops, 128,000m, £8,000	500SL 1985 FSH, 2 onrs, 34,000m, £16,000
380SL 1981 H/S tops, 53,000 miles, £12,000	420SL 1988 FSH, 74,000 miles, £15,000
500SL 1984 H/S tops, 98,000m, £12,500	500SL 1988 FMBSH, 49,000 miles, £15,250
280SL 1985 FMBSH, 70,000 miles, £12,750	300SL 1989 2 onrs, 43,000 miles, £19,500

560SL

A dash of class

WHEN ONE OF the Mercedes-Benz 560SL's newer rivals was introduced a few years ago, some writers dubbed it the "German Corvette." Nonsense. *This*, friends, is the German Corvette. A 1957 Corvette no less.

Corvettes of that period tended to be cranky beasts with more horsepower than handling, but were also great fun and have gone on to become collectors' items. Delete the crankiness, and you're left with the makings of a 560SL.

You have doubts? How else would you describe a 2-seat convertible with a fuel-injected V-8 engine, 4-speed transmission (albeit an automatic), and a chassis that, at times, is more flexible than its suspension?

One can almost hear the Corvette engineers saying, "Hell, we did that years ago."

So did Mercedes-Benz. This is, after all, a design that first appeared in 1971, replacing the rather less energetic 250SL, which in turn replaced (after a suitable interval for mourning) the legendary but flawed 300SL. In any case, a successful 19-year production life is rather beyond the norm, and a tribute to the German obsession with Getting It Right.

Details have changed during the years, to the point where this final iteration of the familiar SL design—due to be superseded any day now by a new SL of up-to-the-minute specification and, one suspects, a truly staggering price tag—is stuffed with every contemporary M-B item in the book. In spite of the updates, the 560

remains a magnificent dinosaur, a relic that combines a kind of haughty gentility with a dash of ruffianism.

That is, I suppose, rather a strange position to take when analyzing a near-$70,000 touring car, but if you ignore the price (hard to do) and the use to which all too many 560s are put (parading in front of the proletariat), what's left is, to a great extent, a Stuttgart street rod.

Example: the healthy and willing 5.5-liter V-8 engine stuffed under that bulging hood. As you might expect, it can be idled along without protest or undue noise, yet a strong push with the right foot provokes a major change in character. What was a silent partner becomes a 227-bhp monster, apparently exhaling through nothing more than a pair of Teutonic Glass-Packs. And while

making sounds you'd associate with Geoff Bodine rather than Hans Herrmann, the engine is pushing the heavy 560 along at a most undignified pace. Some may disagree—the times and speeds recorded for the data panel put the SL well behind stalwarts like the Camaro IROC-Z—but the *feel* is there.

Of course, the big V-8 does have one bad habit: It drinks while you drive. Any major application of power sends the needle on the "economy" gauge scampering for its red zone. In objective terms, that means the SL's fuel mileage will drop below its 16-mpg average. Healthy engines have similarly healthy appetites.

Another example: In deference to the Rodeo Drive cowboys who buy so many SLs, an automatic transmission is all that's available. But this automatic is no slushbox; upshifts are smooth enough not to disturb cruisers, yet crisp enough to please enthusiasts. Even more commendable is the downshifting; at anything up to about 65 mph, full throttle brings an immediate drop from 4th to 2nd, with subsequent upchanges taking place right at the engine's 6000-rpm limit. A clearly defined gate for the shift lever helps when the driver wants to take control, though that's seldom necessary.

One of the many upgrades given the SL during its life is the addition of ABS to the 4-wheel-disc brakes. If these were merely excellent before, they are now beyond reproach. Use the brakes as hard and often as you like; they won't let you down.

It must be said, however, that serious drivers may find the 560's handling less than ideal. Excessive body roll prevails, as in some other super-attenuated suspension layouts, making fast cornering a bit of a trial. Awkward weight transfer and what feels like a small amount of chassis flex add to the problem, robbing the steering and suspension of the precision they display at lower speeds. Ignore these annoyances and the SL will make short work of turns.

Which, you may justifiably point out, means we were asking the Mercedes to perform in circumstances for which it was not intended. Guilty as charged. But certain elements of the car's makeup shout "sports car!" and it's difficult for anyone who is addicted to fast cars to deny them.

It may also be said that these deficiencies are curable, and that's true too. Suspension modifications are available from outside sources; they, along with wider rubber, should make the SL perform like . . . a 1957 Corvette. What that means, for those of you whose experience with great handling comes from slot cars like the Toyota MR2, is great gobs of oversteer, which may not seem like the ideal solution. It isn't. Nonetheless, Sideways Motoring is good for the soul. And the reflexes.

Driven more calmly, the 560SL needs no apologies. As said before, the engine and transmission take light duty in their stride. In addition, the ride is comfortable, and the inte-

Boxy shape (or is it the 3-pointed star?) is still chic for the Eighties. Helpful for gaining entrance to some social circles.

rior cossets it inhabitants with leather, fine carpeting and glossy wood trim. Even suitcases and bags have been given considerate treatment: as befits a first-class touring car, a well-trimmed luggage space has been provided, enough to handle the requirements of a good long trip.

Much of the hardware found in the SL cockpit comes from newer Mercedes-Benzes, but the overall result does not disguise the classic German sports car design. As has become traditional, a large-diameter steering wheel confronts the driver, though it now holds an airbag in its hub; likewise, oversized round dials are graphically equivalent to Mercedes' latest, but somehow seem closer in spirit to 300SL than 300E.

Seating, as in other Mercedes products, draws mixed reviews. For touring, the chairs are well-shaped and comfortable, even if the leather is a bit stiff, but lateral support is lacking. Seatback and fore-aft adjustments are all effected manually, which is not a real hardship; a comfortable position is easy to find.

Another manual operation you might not expect in so expensive a car is the raising and lowering of the fabric top. Nevertheless, when rain clouds appear, it's do-it-yourself time. Fortunately, no great effort is involved; in fact, it takes longer to read about the procedures involved than to perform them.

Raised, the top rattles a bit and lets some wind noise in, but—if a trip through the car wash is any indication—it's leakproof. Lowered, the top resides under a sheet-metal boot. There is also a metal hardtop that comes with each 560, but I left this with Mercedes-Benz; it takes two fairly strong people to lift it and demands storage space when removed.

Age is considered to be good for wines and bad for cars; the 560 is an exception. Inside and out, its design has all the features that might be termed "classic:" lines that are more elegant than aerodynamic, and lots of bright trim everywhere. By the time a later generation of cars entered production, designers knew how to integrate government-mandated safety items; not so for the SL, which looks most dated at its ends, thanks to the oversized bumpers that weren't being called for in 1971.

Otherwise, the body is nicely proportioned and attractive in a manner unaffected by the year-to-year fads some other manufacturers follow. Time has been kind to the SL. It offers performance in the grand manner, there being no substitute for cubic inches when all is said and done (albeit with the traditional drawback of thirst to consider), luxurious accommodations for two, and timeless good looks. And the SL will probably be as nice to drive in the year 2018 as it is today.

Finally, one cannot write about Mercedes-Benz cars without mentioning the Investment Factor. With few exceptions, previous Mercedes have retained their value; more than a few are now worth considerably more than their original cost. Expect that to happen with the 560SL. That may not be the best reason for buying one; it does make the price easier to justify. But don't worry about justification. The 560 can stand on its own four wheels as a high-quality, high-performance touring car with few current rivals.

Can the same be said for Krugerrands? —Ray Thursby

R O A D   T E S T   D A T A

560SL

List price, all POE (1988) **$62,110**
Price as tested ..... (1988) **$63,975**
Price as tested includes std equip.:
(ABS), gas-guzzler tax ($1300), West Coast base price differential ($565)

CHASSIS & BODY

Layout .... front engine/rear drive
Body/frame .... unit steel
Brake system, f/r ....10.9-in. vented
discs/11.0-in. vented discs,
vacuum assist, ABS
Wheels .... cast alloy, 15 x 7J
Tires ....Pirelli P6, 205/65VR-15
Steering type .... recirc ball,
power assist
Turns, lock to lock 3.0
Turning circle, ft 35.2
Suspension, f/r: unequal-length A-arms, coil springs, tube shocks, anti-roll bar/ semi-trailing arms, coil springs, tube shocks, torque compensator, anti-roll bar

GENERAL

Curb weight, lb 3570
Test weight 3720
Wt dist (w/driver), f/r, % 52/48
Wheelbase, in. 96.7
Track, f/r 57.7/57.7
Length 180.3
Width 70.5
Height 51.1
Trunk space, cu ft ...... 9.4 + 5.8
Fuel capacity, U.S. gal. 22.5

ENGINE

Type .... sohc V-8
Bore x stroke, mm ......96.5 x 94.8
Displacement, cc 5547
Compression ratio 9.0:1
Bhp @ rpm, SAE net ...227 @ 4750
Torque @ rpm, lb-ft .....279 @ 3250
Fuel injection .... mechanical port
Fuel requirement .... unleaded, 91-pump oct

DRIVETRAIN

Transmission .... 4-sp automatic
Gear ratios: 4th (1.00) 2.47:1
3rd (1.44) 3.56:1
2nd (2.41) 5.95:1
1st (3.68) 9.09:1
1st (3.68 x 1.90) 17.27:1
Final-drive ratio 2.47:1

ACCELERATION

Time to distance, sec:
0–100 ft 3.3
0–500 ft 8.4
0–1320 ft (¼ mi) 15.2
Speed at end of ¼ mi, mph 90.0
Time to speed, sec:
0–30 mph 2.7
0–60 mph 6.8
0–80 mph 11.5

BRAKING

Minimum stopping distances, ft:
From 60 mph 130
From 80 mph 231
Control in panic stop .... excellent
Overall brake rating .... excellent

HANDLING

Lateral accel, 100-ft radius, g .. 0.78
Speed thru 700-ft
slalom, mph 60.1

SPEEDS IN GEARS

Maximum engine rpm 6000
4th gear (rpm) mph, est (4200) 137
3rd (6000) 118
2nd (6000) 75
1st (6000) 49

CALCULATED DATA

Lb/bhp (test weight) 16.4
Bhp/liter 40.9
Engine revs @ 60 mph in
4th gear 2110
R&T steering index 1.06

INTERIOR NOISE

Idle in neutral, dBA 46
Maximum, 1st gear 78
Constant 70 mph 76

FUEL ECONOMY

Normal driving, mpg 16.5

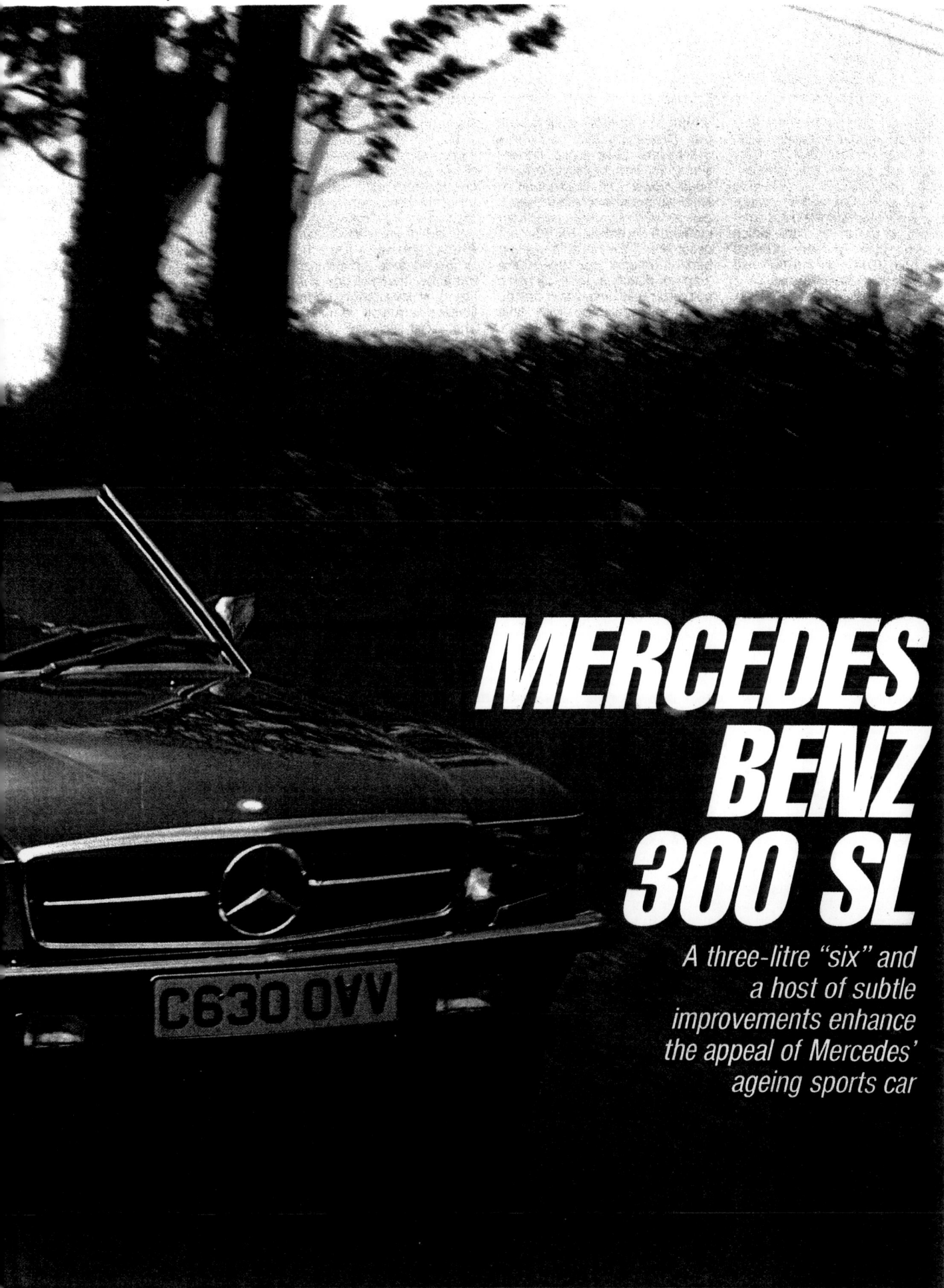

MERCEDES BENZ 300 SL

A three-litre "six" and
a host of subtle
improvements enhance
the appeal of Mercedes'
ageing sports car

C630 OVV

The first Mercedes-Benz sports car to carry the SL tag was the 300 SL. Very quick and very striking, particularly in its gull-wing coupé form, this tricky, swing-axled monster was the least compromised in an SL line which became steadily more civilised over the years and through two major sheet metal changes.

So why hark back to the 300, when it died in 1962? Simply because there is, once again, a 300 SL. It's one of three revised SL models – the other two are the 420 and the 500, both with V8 engines, though there is no sign yet of a 560 version – and it features the new sohc straight-six engine first seen in the 300E version of the W124.

And, more than with most cars perhaps, a look back at SL history is instructive. After all, the current shape, with its concave-roofed hardtop, has been around now for 15 years. Talk Mercedes-Benz and you're talking long time-scales. How much longer this institution of a sports car can continue is a matter of speculation: it can no longer be called evergreen, for it is beginning to go a little brown around the edges.

But, pending the likely introduction of an all-new SL in a year or two, the ageing process has meanwhile been countered by the new engine range. There have been some other updates, too: flush-surfaced alloy wheels (in the new, corporate M-B style) carrying lower-profile 205/65 VR 15 tyres, a revised front spoiler of polycarbonate which reduces front axle lift by 30 per cent, modified front suspension geometry with reduced steering offset, bigger front brake discs with four-pot calipers, new door handles similar to those fitted to the saloons, and minor interior changes including seats with more pronounced curvature. Notable by their absence, though, are the recessed wipers shielded by a raised rear bonnet line, plus the smooth plastic front bumper/spoiler spotted on test in Germany some time back and slated for this latest facelift.

Mercedes-Benz SL motoring doesn't come cheaply. But when you consider that you could spend £31,720 on a 500 SL, the 300 SL at £24,480 seems almost a bargain even if it does cost 15.9 per cent more than did the ousted twin-cam 280 SL.

The new engine remains faithful to Bosch K-Jetronic fuel injection, with which it yields 188 bhp at 5700 rpm and 191 lb ft of torque at a somewhat high 4400 rpm. Displacing 2962 cc with its oversquare bore/stroke dimensions, the iron block/aluminium head power unit is unusual in employing a chain rather than a belt to drive its single overhead camshaft. Hydraulic tappets are used, and the electronic ignition pack contains an alternative map to match it to a catalytic converter – an item which can be fitted retrospectively with little loss in performance.

In view of the 300 SL's all-up weight of just under 30 cwt (1475 kg) 188 bhp provides adequate, rather than startling, performance. The top speed of 123 mph is slower than the class norm by some margin. The Porsche 911 Cabrio, for instance, streaks ahead by no less than 30 mph, the 3.6 XJS and BMW 635 by 14 mph, and the quattro by 5 mph, but then all except the Porsche 944 Lux have considerably more powerful engines. The modest 191 lb ft of torque, especially at a high 4400 rpm, doesn't help here either and although, on the road, the four-speed automatic's responsiveness is a considerable aid, the 300 SL's acceleration times lag behind the rivals. Unsurprisingly the 213 bhp Porsche Cabrio wins the 60 mph sprint taking a mere 5.7 sec, but the Mercedes' 8.4 sec effort is a good second slower than the times returned by the 944 Lux and XJS 3.6, and nearly 2 seconds adrift of the BMW 635's and Audi quattro's times. Despite this, the car feels a good deal quicker on the road than the figures would suggest, helped considerably by the engine's willingness to pull its rev-limited 6200 rpm maximum engine speed. The single overhead cam Mercedes six is at least the equal of BMW's much-respected sixes for smoothness.

The ZF four-speed gearbox makes excellent use of the engine's power. First gear will only engage from rest if the accelerator is pressed firmly, and only then when the "sporting" rather than economy mode is selected. A smart getaway will see the shift to second occur at 5500 rpm, but thereafter the gearbox changes just a whisker short of the rev limiter's intrusion at 6200 rpm. The changes are supremely smooth, even on part throttle, and the box responds instantly when acceleration is demanded, shifting on part throttle, and then again on kickdown, provided the speed is low enough for that particular gear. There is also plenty of bite when the shift occurs and no embarrassing flaring of revs when pulling out to overtake. The short gearing (21.3 mph/1000 rpm) is acceptable too, because the engine is so smooth and quiet.

An overall fuel consumption of 18.4 mpg, however, is disappointing, especially as the car is slower than our selected opposition. The Porsche brigade are considerably more frugal. Even the storming 911 Cabrio can manage 22.2 mpg and the 944 a miserly 24.8 mpg. The turbo quattro has an advantage at the pumps, too, exactly matching the air-cooled 911's thirst. Only the 3.6-litre XJS will guzzle gas at a similar rate: 18.9 mpg.

Broadly speaking, the 300 SL has impeccable manners but in fast cornering it can feel less than sporting. At the front there are double wishbones and coil springs, while at the rear a massive pair of trailing arms, which also incorporate the rear uprights and stub axles, are the basis of the independent rear suspension. Wheel travel feels limited at the rear but despite th the car has a tendency to squ both under power and wh cornering.

The front suspension on t other hand has a much grea travel and feels more sof sprung, so from the rearwa seating position, the bonnet a pears to nod and wallow alor sweeping undulations. It's n unpleasant, but neither is it ta and sporting. Grip from the f 205/65 VR 15 tyres is prodigio and although the the car ten to lean and squat at the sar time, it is possible to cov ground extremely quickly ar safely, aided by supremely dire steering which needs only 2. turns lock to lock. Although tl assistance is subtle, tl weighting stays constant, irr spective of speed or lock, whic does rob the driver of some roa feedback. This is all exacerbate by a huge steering wheel whic manages to rub your knees wh still obscuring the rev counter.

You need to be travelling ve fast indeed before either end w unstick, but it is the front whic starts the trend, with gentle u dersteer building up with spee Only when the power is cut su denly in mid-corner does the sir ple nature of the rear suspensic manifest itself with swift, thoug safe, tightening of line. Real ta out motoring takes a concerte effort by the driver and the so feel of the car tends to deter suc progress anyway. Even if the re suspension is simple in concep it's extremely well sorted ar traction is outstanding. On w roads, full throttle exits from road junction produce r wheelspin or sliding about.

High-speed stability is le good, especially in cross wine and high-speed progress in tra fic can require concentration, e

the facia, differ little from the current Mercedes norm.

Few of our testers could get completely comfortable behind that big wheel, though. As well as being cumbersome to handle, it leaves insufficient room between the bottom of its rim and the cushion for the seat's height adjustment to be of much practical value. It also makes getting out awkward, especially for the broad of beam. The firmly padded seats offer good thigh and lumbar support and push back far enough to accommodate the longest-limbed of drivers, but hard cornering reveals a surprising lack of lateral support. The optional token rear seats can be used to transport one adult or two small children in an emergency but the normally specified luggage platform makes more

pecially as it is such a wide car.

The driver is always aware that this is a big, heavy car, and the ride is appropriately smooth. Very severe bumps can cause the rear suspension to check abruptly, but the suspension travel is extremely well damped. Even so, ride quality falls short of the standard set by the longer wheelbase SEC variants.

The discs all-round, ventilated at the front, are extremely powerful and displayed no signs of fade during repeated hard stops. It is also a compliment to the effectiveness of standard fitment ABS, too, that its existence is never apparent from the feel of the pedal until it is actually working. Pedal weight suffers a little from over-zealous servo assistance but, on the whole, the brakes are excellent.

Inevitably, the greatest source of noise in the cabin comes from the wind, because of the difficulty of sealing even a substantial re-

movable hard top. At high speeds it can become wearing, emanating, in particular, from just behind the occupant's shoulders. But at a more restrained gait it is perfectly acceptable even by saloon standards. With the top removed, wind buffeting is low and the consequent loss of shell stiffness occasions only a marginal increase in scuttle shake, an affliction which is only barely apparent anyway. Road roar from the fat tyres and bump thump are extremely well suppressed, while the engine hardly ever announces its presence, even when extended towards the red line.

The SL's cabin has remained as impervious to fashion as its external styling. Apart from the absurdly large steering wheel, however, there is little that is old fashioned about the ergonomics which, with a single column stalk, a rotary knob for the lights and minor switches in the centre of

Below left: Big single overhead cam straight six is smooth, refined and powerful. Below: Hood is beautifully made, taut and leak-proof

MOTOR ROAD TEST
MERCEDES-BENZ 300SL

PERFORMANCE

WEATHER CONDITIONS

Wind	18 mph
Temperature	52 deg F/11 deg C
Barometer	29.6 in Hg/1003 mbar
Surface	Dry tarmacadam

MAXIMUM SPEEDS

	mph	kph
Banked Circuit (4th gear)	122.8	197.6
Best ¼ mile (4th gear)	126.0	202.8
Terminal speeds:		
at ¼ mile	84	135
at kilometre	107	172
Speeds in gears (at 6200 rpm):		
1st†	32	51
2nd	55	88
3rd	92	148

†At 5500 rpm

ACCELERATION FROM REST

mph	sec	kph	sec
0-30	3.0	0-40	2.5
0-40	4.4	0-60	4.0
0-50	6.1	0-80	6.1
0-60	8.4	0-100	9.0
0-70	11.2	0-120	12.7
0-80	14.5	0-140	17.7
0-90	18.9	0-160	24.1
0-100	24.6		
Stand'g ¼	16.5	Stdg km	30.2

ACCELERATION IN KICKDOWN

mph	sec	kph	sec
20-40	2.5	40-60	1.5
30-50	3.1	60-80	2.1
40-60	4.0	80-100	2.9
50-70	5.1	100-120	3.7
60-80	6.1	120-140	5.0
70-90	7.7	140-160	6.4
80-100	10.1		

FUEL CONSUMPTION

Overall	18.4 mpg
	15.4 litres/100 km
Touring*	23.7 mpg
	11.9 litres/100 km

Govt tests	20.2 mpg (urban)
	30.0 mpg (56 mph)
	24.4 mpg (75 mph)
Fuel grade	97 octane
	4 star rating
Tank capacity	85 litres
	18.7 galls
Max range*	443 miles
	713 km
Test distance	723 miles
	1164 km

*Based on official fuel economy figures – 50 per cent of urban cycle, plus 25 per cent of each of 56/75 mph consumptions.

STEERING

Turning circle	10.3 m 33.8 ft
Lock to lock	2.8 turns

NOISE

	dBA
30 mph	63
50 mph	67
70 mph	73
Maximum†	78

†Peak noise level under full-throttle acceleration in 2nd

SPEEDOMETER (MPH)

True mph	30	40	50	60	70	80	90	100
Speedo	32	44	52	61	70	81	92	100

Distance recorder: 2.0 per cent fast

WEIGHT

	Kg	cwt
Unladen weight*	1475	29.0
Weight as tested	1690	33.3

*No fuel

Performance tests carried out by *Motor*'s staff at the Motor Industry Research Association proving ground, Lindley, and Millbrook proving ground, near Ampthill.

Test Data: World Copyright reserved. No reproduction in whole or part without written permission.

GENERAL SPECIFICATION

ENGINE

Cylinders	6-in-line
Capacity	2962 cc
Bore/stroke	88.5/80.3 mm
Max power	188 bhp (138 kW) at 5700 rpm (DIN)
Max torque	192 lb ft (260 Nm) at 4400 rpm (DIN)
Block	Cast iron
Head	Aluminium alloy
Cooling	Water
Valve gear	Sohc chain drive, hydraulic tappets, 2 valves per cylinder
Compression	9.2:1
Fuel system	Bosch KE-Jetronic mechanical
Ignition	Fully programmed electronic
Bearings	Seven main

TRANSMISSION

Drive	To rear wheels
Type	Four-speed manual

Internal ratios and mph/1000 rpm

4th	1.00/21.3
3rd	1.44/14.8
2nd	2.41/8.8
1st	3.68/5.8
Rev	4.22
Final drive	3.46:1

AERODYNAMICS

Cd	0.41

SUSPENSION

Front	Independent by double wishbones, coil springs, anti-roll bar.
Rear	Independent by semi- trailing arms, coil springs, anti-roll bar.

STEERING

Type	Recirculating ball
Assistance	Yes

BRAKES

Front	Ventilated Discs 28.4 cm dia
Rear	Discs, 27.9 cm dia
Servo	Yes
Circuit	Split front/rear
Rear valve	No – ABS anti-lock brakes fitted standard

WHEELS/TYRES

Type	Aluminium alloy 7J × 15 in dia
Tyres	205/65 VR15
Pressures F/R (normal)	29/35 psi 2.0/2.4 bar
(full load/high speed)	32/36 psi 2.2/2.5 bar

ELECTRICAL

Battery	12 v, 62 Ah
Alternator	70 Amp
Fuses	20
Headlights type	Halogen
dip	110 W total
main	130 W total

GUARANTEE

Duration	12 months unlimited.
Rust warranty	None

MAINTENANCE

Major service	12,000 miles
Intermediate service	6,000 miles

Make: Mercedes-Benz Model: 300 SL Country of Origin: West Germany
Maker: Daimler Benz, Stuttgart. UK Concessionaire: Mercedes-Benz (UK) Ltd, Delaware Drive, Tongwell, Milton Keynes MK15 8HA
Tel: 0908 668899 Total Price: £24,840 Options: Air conditioning £1514, Air bag £956, Leather seats £663, Metallic paint £454, Radio £632, Rear child seats £320, Cruise control £232.

Above: Facia has hardly changed in 15 years – wheel is still absurdly big. Left: Likewise the instrumentation which is clear and comprehensive. Below left: Front seats offer good lumbar support. Below: Token rear seats are just that

sense in two-seater touring, augmenting the modest 0.19m³ capacity of the boot.

Removing the beautifully made steel hardtop requires the efforts of two people but, since there are just four mounting lugs, the operation takes only a matter of seconds. Erecting the equally superb hood is relatively simple, too, and in place it feels rigid and taut. The hood's thick rear three-quarter panels create more of a blind spot at acutely-angled T-junctions than the hard top's but visibility is generally good, aided by efficient wipers, though the headlights are disappointingly feeble.

For the rest, the SL is much as it has always been. The instruments are large, clear and boldly marked, the easily-regulated heating complemented by powerful face-level ventilation and the standards of build and finish beyond reproach, if somewhat short on design flair.

The 300 SL isn't over-burdened with equipment, either, lacking both a radio/cassette (£632 extra) and a cruise control (£232), though electric window lifters and central locking do come as standard. At £24,480, it's up against rivals that are better appointed, faster or both. The line-up includes Jaguar's XJS 3.6 Cabrio (£22,395), BMW's 635 CSi (£27,995), Porsche's 911 Carrera Cabrio (£29,253) and 944 Lux (£20,275) and the Audi quattro (£24,204) which, along with the 911, is the only rival not available with automatic transmission.

But out-and-out speed merchants have never clamoured for the SL. The 300 SL's top speed, after all, is matched by the Renault 5 GT Turbo's at around a third of the price. This convertible Merc is only as quick as it needs to be to exhilarate with the hood down. The rest of the experience is far more subtle and long-lasting, based as much on build and engineering elegance as seat-of-the-pants driver satisfaction.

At the end of the day, this is a good Mercedes and a good rag top. For some, the combination will always be irresistible.

MERCEDES-BENZ 300 SL

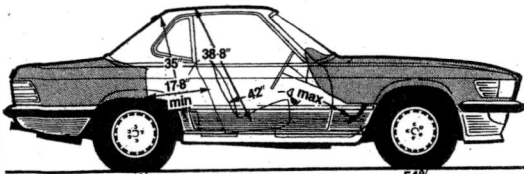

£24,840

Capacity, cc	2962
Power bhp/rpm	188/5700
Torque lb ft/rpm	192/4400
Max speed, mph	122.8
0-60 mph, sec	8.4
30-50 mph in 4th, sec	3.1
mph/1000 rpm	21.3
Overall mpg	18.4
Touring mpg	23.7
Weight kg	1475
Drag coefficient Cd	0.41
Boot capacity m³	0.19

New six-cylinder version of Mercedes' ageing convertible is no standard-setter but packs a lot of appeal into a still elegant shape. Smooth, willing engine is mated to superbly responsive 4-speed auto and, up to 100 mph, performance is strong. No prizes for economy, though, and SL feels rather dated from behind the overlarge wheel. Handling is safe, grip impressive and ride comfortable, but equipment is sparse for £25,000. Superbly built and finished, nonetheless.

Length 4·39m (172·8″)   Width 1·78m (70·3″)   Front track 1·45m (57″)
Wheelbase 2·46m (96·8″)   Height 1·34m (52·8″)   Rear track 1·45m (57·3″)

BMW 635 CSi

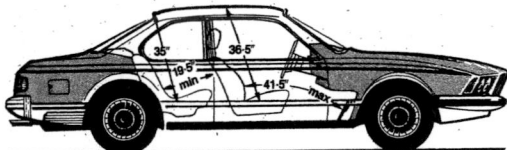

£27,995

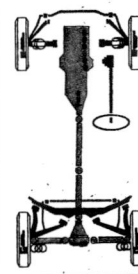

Capacity, cc	3430
Power bhp/rpm	218/5200
Torque lb ft/rpm	229/4000
Max speed, mph	137.1
0-60 mph, sec	6.9
30-50 mph in 4th, sec	7.2
mph/1000 rpm	28.9
Overall mpg	22.5
Touring mpg	26.8
Weight kg	1415
Drag coefficient Cd	N/A
Boot capacity m³	0.36

BMW's sleek 635CSi is rapid and refined in its latest form, and sets high standards of economy in the supercoupé class. Handling and dry road grip are excellent, too, though in the wet traction is poor and the tail needs watching. Comfortable ride, superb gearchange, anti-lock brakes are further plus points, but rear accommodation, as in Jag, is cramped. Tested as a manual but also available with dual-mode, four-speed automatic.

Length 4·75m (187″)   Width 1·73m (68″)   Front track 1·42m (56″)
Wheelbase 2·62m (103″)   Height 1·37m (54″)   Rear track 1·46m (57·5″)

AUDI QUATTRO

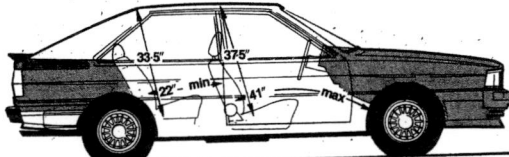

£23,273

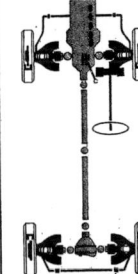

Capacity, cc	2144
Power bhp/rpm	200/5500
Torque lb ft/rpm	210/3500
Max speed, mph	131.7
0-60 mph, sec	6.5
30-50 mph in 4th, sec	8.2
mph/1000 rpm	22.2
Overall mpg	18.7
Touring mpg	24.5
Weight kg	1250
Drag coefficient Cd	0.43
Boot capacity m³	0.22

A more civilised machine these days than its epoch-making predecessor, the 4wd Quattro is more than ever a milestone in car design. It combines phenomenal roadholding and traction with performance, refinement, economy, comfort and accommodation in a way that has no equal, against which its weaknesses – poor ratios (still) and slow shift, unprogressive heating, sparse instruments – are minor failings. Now with anti-lock braking as standard.

Length 4·40m (173·3″)   Width 1·72m (67·8″)   Front track 1·45m (57·3″)
Wheelbase 2·52m (99·3″)   Height 1·34m (53″)   Rear track 1·42m (56″)

JAGUAR XJSC 3.6 Cabrio

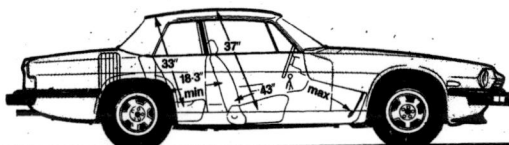

£22,395

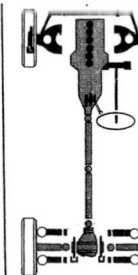

Capacity, cc	3590
Power bhp/rpm	225/5300
Torque lb ft/rpm	240/4000
Max speed, mph	136.8
0-60 mph, sec	7.2
30-50 mph in 4th, sec	6.9
mph/1000 rpm	28.9
Overall mpg	18.9
Touring mpg	24.2
Weight kg	1645
Drag coefficient Cd	0.41
Boot capacity m³	0.31

Jaguar's smaller-engined six-cylinder XJS excels in most areas but is badly disappointing in the most important one of all. Its 3.6-litre AJ6 engine, while a lusty performer, is neither as smooth nor as economical as it should be. Otherwise it's good news: a positive gearchange, a beautifully balanced chassis with good grip and a superb ride, fine finish and appointments. Still a desirable 2+2, but could be so much better. The Cabrio's hood is awkward to operate.

Length 4·87m (191·8″)   Width 1·79m (10·5″)   Front track 1·47m (58″)
Wheelbase 2·59m (102″)   Height 1·26m (49·8″)   Rear track 1·48m (58·5″)

PORSCHE 944 LUX

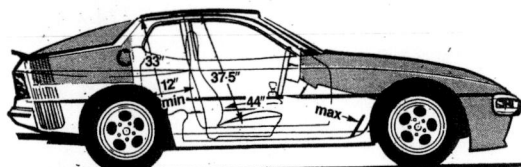

£18,234

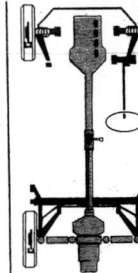

Capacity, cc	2479
Power bhp/rpm	163/5800
Torque lb ft/rpm	151/3000
Max speed, mph	137*
0-60 mph, sec	7.2
30-50 mph in 4th, sec	6.2
mph/1000 rpm	22.8
Overall mpg	24.8
Touring mpg	30.6
Weight kg	1135
Drag coefficient Cd	0.33
Boot capacity m³	0.14
*Estimated	

Propelled by a supremely smooth big "four" which sets high standards of fuel efficiency for a high performance sports car, the 944 is a lusty performer, and has the roadholding and brakes to match, though its handling takes some taming once you overstep its limits. Fine gearchange and good driving position further underline its driver appeal and recent interior re-vamp included better heating and ventilation. Road noise is excessive over poor surfaces.

Length 4·21m (166″)   Width 1·73m (68·3″)   Front track 1·48m (58·3″)
Wheelbase 2·40m (94·5″)   Height 1·27m (50″)   Rear track 1·44m (57″)

PORSCHE 911 Carrera Cabrio

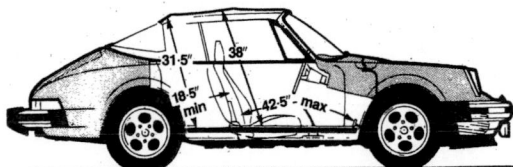

£29,253

Capacity, cc	3164
Power bhp/rpm	231/5900
Torque lb ft/rpm	209/4800
Max speed, mph	152.2
0-60 mph, sec	5.7
30-50 mph in 4th, sec	5.8
mph/1000 rpm	23.2
Overall mpg	21.1
Touring mpg	28.6
Weight kg	1155
Drag coefficient Cd	0.40
Boot capacity m³	0.28

The 911 Carrera Cabriolet ranks as one of the most impressive open cars ever made. Superb 3.2-litre flat six delivers storming acceleration and 152 mph top speed yet returns more than 20 mpg. Tremendous handling becomes tricky in the wet and ride is very firm around town, but as a practical day-to-day supercar, the Porsche has no peers. Hood is beautifully made (in keeping with the excellent build), and easy to use.

Length 4·29m (169″)   Width 1·65m (65″)   Front track 1·43m (56·3″)
Wheelbase 2·27m (89·5″)   Height 1·31m (51·8″)   Rear track 1·49m (59″)

Mercedes Benz W129 SL500
Silver Arrow

S'LONG

Merc's classy roadster gets the elbow later
this year. We pay our respects with a blast
across country in the final special edition

STORY ANDREW FRANKEL PHOTOGRAPHS PETE GIBSON

Mercedes Benz W129 SL500
Silver Arrow

It was a chance reunion. Until the last minute someone else was going to drive this, the last of the current generation of Mercedes SL and I would never have seen it there, gleaming silver in the sunshine as if it had never been away.

This luxury rag-top is an old friend, you see. In fact it's been 12 years since our last brief encounter. Back then we were both bright young things, united by enthusiasm for the life and road ahead. But now we have grown up and put on weight. I have the dubious delights of middle age to look forward to, but compared to the alternative that awaits this SL I feel that I'm in no position to complain.

I am pleased that the SL still looks good, despite the visible signs of age beneath the AMG cosmetic slap designed to preserve its youth long enough for one last hurrah. For this is the SL 'Silver Arrow', the ultimate run out special, a £68,940 valedictory service for a car that was once great but has now outstayed its welcome on our roads.

I wish car companies would desist from pillaging their heritage when applying such names to such cars. The last time I saw a Silver Arrow it was a 1955 W196 Grand Prix car – the machine used by Juan Manuel Fangio to lift consecutive Formula One world championships and to bring Stirling Moss his first Grand Prix victory. This SL may or may not be a fine car but an AMG body, aluminium brightwork, big wheels and a polished exhaust pipe do not a Silver Arrow make. Not in my book at least. But I digress. For a while it is just like old times and I remember at once what drew me to this car in the first place. The 5-litre V8 under the bonnet is new but its 302bhp and, more significantly, the 339lb ft of torque it musters at just 2700rpm smack as much of open road greatness as ever. More than this, though, is the depth of its engineering integrity.

Mercedes rank highly among the best built cars on the road. But this is the best built Mercedes I have driven since my last ride in a previous generation S-class. The hood may not rise and fall as fast as some these days but it still operates with unparalleled grace and precision; the doors feel excessively, gloriously heavy and thunk home like those of no other open car. Beauty, power and integrity – things I fell for 12 years ago.

But now I notice other things that would not have bothered me in my early 20s. For such a large car it is uncommonly mean in its allocation of space, both in the cockpit and boot. And try as I might, I cannot persuade either the seat squab or back to adopt a position that suits my large but hardly freakish frame. As this is a car designed before airbags became de rigeur, it's lost its glovebox too. But I was pleased to note that while age has played

> ## "I fell for its beauty, power and integrity"

its cruel tricks in many areas, it has not wearied the SL. GTi drivers who chance across one – at least one fitted with the five-litre engine – and mistake it for a centre-lane sluggard will soon see their illusions shrinking into the distance. I can remember recording sub-six second 0-60mph runs in the first 500SL I drove and while it is now the SL500 and claims 6.5sec for the slightly longer 0-62mph run, in truth it feels as fast as it ever was.

It means you'll need a Porsche Boxster S even to take a look at that polished exhaust pipe for more than a split second – so respect for this elder and almost certainly better is due and deserved.

Its automatic gearbox now has five gears, although there is no sign of the semi-automatic sequential shift pattern now accepted as the norm among quality autos.

No matter. The SL never was a car for screaming through the gears. Its character calls for a relaxed approach, for the driver to chill out and bathe in the torque. A twiddle of the toe and flex of the wrist are the most demanding tasks on a typical journey. It is a seductive mode of travel for a while, but it is not addictive. For while some of its more modern rivals such as the Porsche 911 and Jaguar XKR cabriolets offer similarly relaxed progress, it is always provided with the promise of a ♦

Despite enormous grip, SL is more cruiser than back-road charger

COMINGSOON

The 12-year-old SL is a dinosaur which will soon be extinct, to be replaced by a bigger, all-new car this autumn. The sleek new SL promises to be a technological tour de force, with electro-hydraulic brakes and Mercedes' active body control suspension, which uses hydraulic cylinders to suppress body roll. The canvas roof will be replaced by a folding hard-top more in keeping with a £60k car, and a sharper rack and pinion system will appear. Power will come from 5.0 and supercharged 5.5-litre V8s, although a 3.2-litre V6 will join the line up later.

Mercedes Benz W129 SL500
Silver Arrow

rather more mentally demanding alternative should the desire to mash the accelerator into the carpet take you. And no amount of cosmetic surgery will disguise the SL's age. It simply cannot keep up with a hard-driven rival. Nor does it appear remotely minded to try.

It's not that it lacks the basic requirements of a rapid car. It's capable of straight-line speeds not all that far short of either the Porsche or Jaguar. And the monster 275/40 ZR 18 tyres that clothe the 9.5in rear wheels deliver compelling grip. But the driving experience itself simply doesn't match up to the SL's abundant performance potential.

If your reaction to the news that this car has 1980s steering is to ask what I was expecting from a car designed in that decade, all I would counter is that it is still surprising and almost shocking to see how far we have come in the intervening years. The Mercedes' system is vague and bereft of feel. It discourages you from going faster not because the car feels even remotely unsafe but, more prosaically, because the traditional rewards of such endeavours are notable only by their absence. Steering this car is not a tactile delight. Furthermore, if you really want to thunder across the scenery, you will discover only modest body control and a degree of scuttle shake you'd never encounter in an SLK. The SL reacts to being worked hard with the benevolent horror of one who has seen it all before, was once mildly amused by it but today, and all other things being equal, would rather be doing something altogether less childish instead.

How does it feel to play the SL's game? Turn on the cruise control on the dash and in your brain, waft rather than charge

Much of the Silver Arrow's detailing now showing its age; dash gets classy retro treatment, though

Engine's 302bhp, allied to 339lb ft of torque available at 2700rpm, give the heavy SL blistering pace

Three-pointed star shines again

and suddenly it all makes sense. This is sybaritic transport: it's like a wheeled version of the St Tropez sea front, where little is asked of you other than plenty of money and that you're an afficionado of wind and sun. It rides sublimely well in such situations, manages the air flow in the cockpit extremely efficiently and relaxes you like few cars others can. Suitably ensconced there, take time to appreciate the comfort of the seats, the soft burble of the V8 and, yes, the appreciative stares of the onlookers. It is every inch the convertible of your dreams.

But not mine. Twelve years ago I was too young to be seduced by such charms and I think I'm pleased to note that the same remains true today. The SL was once

SL500 prefers to waft along; scuttle shake and woolly steering put paid to anything more adventurous

Mercedes Benz W129 SL500
Silver Arrow

a great car and even now I'd rate it as good. Something this well engineered and still so effective at that which it professes to do best could never be thought of as anything else.

Yet what kept us as just good friends 12 years ago has done so again today. We're both older and smarter but neither of us has really changed. And, knowing that we will probably meet again, I feel no sense of sorrow at our parting. I enjoyed meeting up again, remembering the old days and how we were in our youth but too soon we had exhausted what we had in common and were left with little more than respectful and polite indifference.

I think this probably says as much about me as the car, as the SL has been incredibly successful for Mercedes and fully deserves the status and plaudits it has acquired over the years. But the time is right for its replacement. There will be only 100 right-hand drive Silver Arrow SLs and doubtless they will be being snapped up as you read these words. And despite the bum note struck by the name, I can't see those owners being less than delighted with their choice. The SL as car and concept has been around long enough for it to be inconceivable that anyone would buy one expecting it to be anything other than what it appears.

But the time has come for Mercedes to bring the world a lighter, lither, more savvy SL. It needs to fulfil the brief of the car it replaces, but also focus much more on the needs and desires of the enthusiast driver. It needs to combine open-top grand-touring glamour and panache with the attributes of a sports car. That, I am hoping, is exactly what the new model will do. I find myself full of anticipation at the prospect of our first meeting. ●

Enormous 18in alloys are part of the end-of-line model's attractions

Factfile

MERCEDES SL500 SILVER ARROW

How much?

Price	£69,940
On sale in UK	Now

How fast?

0-60mph	6.5sec
Top speed	155mph (limited)

How thirsty?

Urban	15.8mpg
Extra urban	33.5mpg
Combined mpg	23.7mpg
CO_2 emissions	300g/km

How big?

Length	4470mm
Width	1812mm
Height	1303mm
Wheelbase	2515mm
Weight	1890kg
Fuel tank	90 litres

Engine

Layout 8 cyls in vee, 4966cc
Max power 302bhp at 5600rpm
Max torque 339lb ft at 2700-4250rpm
Specific output 61bhp per litre
Power to weight 160bhp per tonne
Installation Front, longitudinal, rear-wheel drive
Bore/stroke 97/84mm
Made of All aluminium
Compression ratio 10.0:1
Valve gear 3 per cyl, dohc
Ignition and fuel Electronic ignition, multi-point fuel injection

Gearbox

Type Five-speed automatic
Ratios/mph per 1000rpm

1st 3.6/8.0	2nd 2.2/13.0
3rd 1.4/20.6	4th 1.0/28.7
5th 0.8/35.6	Final drive 2.65

Suspension

Front Struts, wishbones, coil springs, anti-roll bar
Rear Multi-link, coil springs, anti-roll bar

Steering

Type Power assisted recirculating ball
Lock to lock 2.9

Brakes

Front 345mm ventilated discs
Rear 331mm ventilated discs

Wheels and tyres

Size 8.5 x 18in (f), 9.5 x 18in (r)
Made of alloy
Tyres 245/45 ZR18 (f), 275/40 ZR18 (r)

Silver Arrow extras can't disguise the fact that the 12-year old SL is ripe for replacement; special edition sill plate is illuminated at night

TWIN TEST
MERCEDES SL600 v SL60 AMG

THE RAW AND
THE CO

At first glance, the sublime SL600 looks as much Mercedes sports car as you'd ever need. But then again, have you clocked the AMG SL60...

SL 60

AMG job will appeal to driving enthusiasts – it's cheaper, too

SL 600

Built to last forever, a breeze to drive, more pull than Brad Pitt

A mainstay of hard core German tuning firms, the Mercedes SL is a car you can cut to suit your needs. Almost nothing is too extreme if you have deep enough pockets and industrial-strength neck muscles.

The big, angular convertible – arguably some way past its glory days, though still selling well post SLK – clearly has engineering and build integrity to spare. The widely accepted notion is that the tuning outfits merely take up the slack; work the design that little bit harder.

Maybe so but, let's be absolutely honest here, where's the ▶

Driver and passenger airbags are standard on SL60 (pic) and SL600

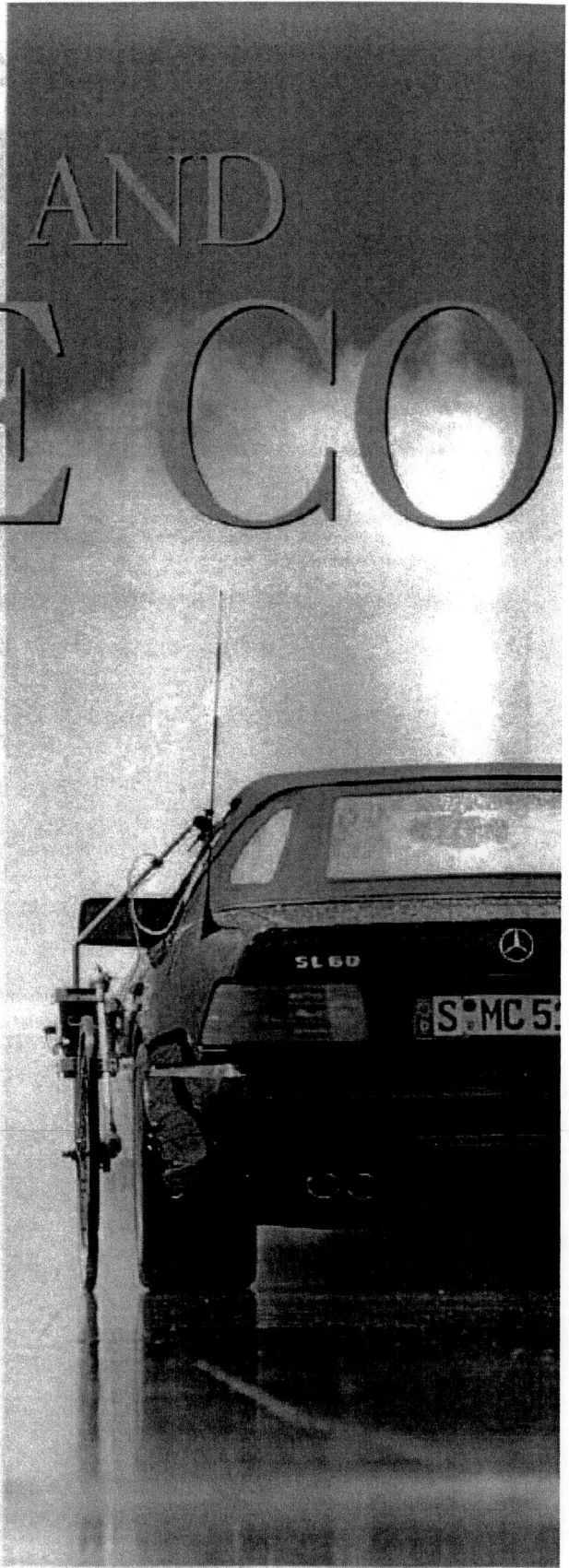

Mercedes Benz SL60 v SL600
W129 Series

OKED

Lower ride height and monstrous twin pipes mark out the SL60 AMG. SL600 is a more sedate affair, both in looks and dynamics

SL 600

S·MC 5178

AMG

Mercedes Benz SL60 v SL600
W129 Series

scope for underachievement in a car that costs £102,400 and packs a 394bhp 6.0-litre V12 under its bonnet? Exactly.

The SL600, flagship of the 'works' SL range, should be seven shades of wonderful – as much Mercedes sports car as any reasonable person could ever wish for.

And yet there appears to be a tacit admission in the Mercedes price list that it might not quite be everyone's idea of the sublime SL. Because, nestling neatly between it and the £22,000 cheaper 5.0-litre V8 SL500, is the SL60 AMG – to wit, Mercedes' very own tuned 'n' tweaked SL.

It's a rarity, to be sure, but it does sell: Mercedes shifted 19 in the UK in 1996, against 48 SL600s.

The SL60 AMG, too, has a 6.0-litre engine but one that's based on the SL500's V8. Price is a cool £97,450 (£100k-plus if it's equipped to opulent SL600

standards). And, with 381bhp on tap, it possesses the sort of acceleration that's bad for your blood pressure. The urge is heavy-duty and sustained well beyond 100mph while the sixty mark is despatched in just 5.8secs, two tenths ahead of the heavier SL600.

But figures aren't the issue here. Both cars are hugely rapid, the AMG staying fractionally in front from standstill to max. What separates AMG's interpretation of a top SL from Mercedes' own is character. The engines, for instance, could hardly be more different. The SL60 is pure V8, all mellow bellow with just the right hint of aggression from its visible large-bore exhausts (you can't see the SL600's at all). It punches hard from a handful of revs above idle and responds hungrily to the throttle thereafter.

The SL600 is a model of cultured refinement by comparison. Its power delivery is softer, its throttle response slower. This is big power that's fuzzy at the edges – like being pushed along by a hydraulic ram but with a cushion in between.

Chassis contrasts are just as marked. And again, the SL600 is made to feel like a gentleman's tourer by the harder, sharper SL60 which eschews ▶

> 'Both cars are hugely rapid, but the SL600 is still a model of cultured refinement'

MERCEDES SL600

Enormous 6.0-litre V12 knocks out 394bhp at 5,200rpm while peak torque of 420lb ft is delivered at 3,800rpm. Power is put down beautifully, although Mercedes' many traction aids limit the fun somewhat

Mercedes Benz SL60 v SL600
W129 Series

SL60 (pic) is dynamically alive compared with SL600. Buy one and sunny sundays will never be the same again

MERCEDES AMG SL60

The AMG's 6.0-litre V8 is based on the SL500's. A few horses short of the SL600 at 381bhp but car is 100kg lighter and, with 428lb ft on tap, has more torque. Top speed, as with the SL600, is limited to 155mph and 60mph comes in just 5.5secs

Mercedes Benz SL60 v SL600
W129 Series

Chucking around the SL600 is more frustrating than thrilling because of its soft suspension set-up. Engine note is dull, as well

Hard-case alloys tuck in tight thanks to SL60's lowered body

SL600's hi-tech stability system ensures grip even in extremes

> 'SL60 is a real sports car that you can take by the scruff of the neck and drive'

the V12's cosy suppleness for body control that's reminiscent of a Porsche 928's – but without that car's thudding tyre noise.

Not only does the SL60 ride lower and firmer than the SL600, it weighs 100kg less, mostly at the front. This largely explains why it has a more incisive turn-in and changes direction with much greater alacrity.

In general, the SL60 feels more alive and agile than the SL600, which rolls prodigiously by comparison and feels

altogether heavier and lazier. If you are tempted to gun the big V12 through the tight and twisties, it copes. Standard electronic stability programme (ESP) makes it almost impossible to lose it, but the question you find yourself asking is "who would want to try that hard in the first place?" Ease back, enjoy the scenery.

The SL60 doesn't re-write the SL rule book, of course. Its stiffer underpinnings put more energy into a bodyshell that isn't the last word in rigidity with sundry creaks and groans the result. And it doesn't put its power down as well as the SL600; the ASR traction control is constantly butting in and interrupting the flow. For all that, though, the SL60 AMG is a real sports car that you can take by the scruff of the neck and drive.

The Mercedes SL600, by these standards, is just a big old pussycat, after all.

Car VERDICT   SL600 fails the sports test

① MERCEDES SL60 AMG   £97,450   ★★★★★

✓ AMG twigged that the lighter, more nimble SL500 was a better car than its V12-engined big brother so set about building a harder, crisper and more rewarding 500 with even more grunt than the 600. It succeeded. The SL60 goes hard, sounds glorious and handles with bite and precision.

✗ AMG cosmetics are not exactly the last word in understatement. Stiffer suspension surprisingly doesn't harm ride much but does emphasise the less than state-of-the-art body stiffness. Expect creaks and groans on bumpy roads. Apparent price advantage over SL600 down to less standard kit.

② MERCEDES SL600   £102,400   ★★★★

✓ Ultimate 'works' SL. Bit Time acceleration and top speed from one of the world's beefiest V12s puts most traffic into reverse. Has all the comforts and traction aids Mercedes could think of. Comfortable and civilised yet built like a nuclear bunker. Effortless and elegant in all it does.

✗ The SL600 costs £102k so you'd expect it to be fabulous from tip to toe. It isn't. For all its mighty urge, the big V12 never sounds much more interesting than a vacuum cleaner. Soft suspension keeps the ride smooth but kills any idea of ever having fun. A sports car in image only.

SPECIFICATIONS   SL60 the better all-round package

		MERCEDES SL 600	MERCEDES SL 60 AMG
ENGINE			
Capacity	ccm	5,987	5,956
Cylinders		V12	V8
Max power	bhp at rpm	394/5,200	381/5,600
Max torque	lb ft at rpm	420/3,800	428/3,750
Transmission		5-speed automatic	5-speed automatic
DIMENSIONS			
Kerb Weight	kg	1,930	1,884
Length/width/height	mm	4,499/1,812/1,286	4,470/1,812/1,293
Wheelbase		2,515	2,515
Boot volume	litres	260	265
Tyres/wheels		8x16 225/55	8x16 225/55
Brakes (Discs front/rear)		Vented/vented (ABS)	Vented/vented (ABS)
PERFORMANCE			
0-50mph	secs	4.5	4.5
0-60mph		6.0	5.8
0-100mph		13.5	13.1
0-120mph		21.6	21.0
Top speed	mph	155*	155*
BRAKING			
70-0mph (cold/hot)	m	48.0/48.5	47.5/47.5
NOISE LEVELS			
30mph	dB(A)	57	60
60mph		69	68
100mph		79	74
FUEL CONSUMPTION			
Composite	mpg	21.5	21.8
Overall test		18.7	17.6
EQUIPMENT			
Airbag (Driver/passenger)		•/•	•/•
Air conditioning		•	•
Automatic		•	•
CD player		£602	£602
Electric roof		•	•
Electric windows		•	•
Leather upholstery		•	•
Metallic paint		•	•

• Standard   – Not available   *Electronically limited

Mercedes Benz
W230 Series SL500

SUPER ROADSTER
SPECIAL

STORY **PETER ROBINSON** PHOTOGRAPHS **STAN PAPIOR**

TWIN
PEAKS

Mercedes' first all-new SL in more than
a decade sharpens its sporting coupé
as well as its luxury cabriolet credentials

Sometimes you just can't stop driving. Happened to me when I first laid hands on the new SL. Despite the unexpected blue skies and warm sun, I felt oddly tense about trying the first all-new version in 12 years of such a successful formula. But my anxiety – this car has to deliver much if it is to live up to the hype – vanished within 10 minutes of my taking the wheel.

The SL, I discovered, was as good as its promise: predictably excellent on the road, and predictable, too, in the way it updates and significantly improves on the SL's timeless strengths. And all without compromising its essential character. Owners of the current car will be neither disappointed nor surprised by the new model, so obviously a fresh interpretation of such a hugely successful concept. One that, staggeringly enough, no other car maker (Jaguar perhaps excepted) has seriously challenged in close on 40 years.

Tension released, all I want now is to drive the thing. A decade of engineering development has transformed the SL into a lighter-feeling, more agile and sporting machine. There's a nimbleness that's overlaid, as you'd expect, with indulgent levels of comfort. The old car, capable and certainly heavy and solid in a way no modern Mercedes can hope to match, feels aged and staid in comparison.

We're on the twisty, hilly roads south-east of Stuttgart, the same roads on which the SL underwent much of its development. No surprises, then, that the svelte two-seater should feel perfectly at home here, and inspire an intense desire to search out its limits.

You don't drive the SL as you would a Ferrari 360 Modena or even a regular 911. It is so much more laid back – too calming, too soft, altogether too indulgent to match the thrilling alertness and urgency of the Ferrari. Then, just as you begin to suspect the SL's priorities are too heavily ♦

Mercedes Benz
W230 Series SL500

weighted towards effortless cruising, conditions change and it takes on a tougher edge. It's then that you understand that the new SL copes brilliantly with mid-corner bumps and, 5.0-litre V8 mildly bellowing, that it can blast out of corners – proving it can be a cruiser for the blue-rinse set *and* a proper sports car, too. At the end of a long day's driving you want to keep going, and never hand back the keys. Or in this case the keyless entry card.

Mercedes has thrown the entire weight of its technology at the SL. It inherits the electro-hydraulic suspension – called Active Body Control (ABC) – from the CL coupé/S600 and is the first production car in the world to use a brake-by-wire system. The folding steel and glass roof of the

"MERCEDES HAS THROWN TECHNOLOGY AT THE SL"

SL is a complex work of art that takes 16sec to convert from a near silent coupé into a roadster. The ability to be two cars in one is crucial to the car's appeal.

Open the long door and it's obvious Mercedes is going through a revolution in the concept of its interiors. The SL is like no other M-B and offers a preview of next year's E-class. The dashboard separates driver and passenger, flowing gently into a wide central console. A strong circular theme involves the instruments (far fewer than in SLs of old and with Alfa-like circular hoods), four air vents and the controls for the air-conditioning.

Tall drivers will appreciate that extending the wheelbase by 45mm produces an SL with adequate seat travel. Shorter occupants will appreciate the increased cushion height adjustment and the steering wheel's staggering range of reach and rake. The superb seats adjust every which way, and those on the test car offered a massage and cooling ventilation through the cushion.

The cabin, far more spacious than the old model's (except for space behind the seats), and equipped with every luxury item you can imagine, and some you probably can't, presents a confusing array of switches, buttons and controls, including a start-stop button topping the gearlever. The basics are easy, but taking full advantage of the SL's opulence isn't going to be the work of a moment. We counted 14 controls, buttons and switches on the driver's door, nine on each seat and another 96 – yes, 96 – scattered around the dashboard, console and above the interior mirror. And I doubt I found them all.

When first I saw the SL, I reckoned Mercedes had matched the best from Audi, but the interior lacks Ingolstadt's design integration and peerless quality. Nor does the way the boot lid rocks gently on its incredibly complicated system of hinges, inspire confidence in its ability to work trouble-free for the life of the car.

There's much more to the SL than a gimmicky interior, of course. Not least the three valves per cylinder, sohc 302bhp V8. A cultured V8-burble at idle underlines its potential. The engine is not new, but it works brilliantly in the SL; it is effortlessly smooth to the 5800rpm full-throttle change up points dictated by Mercedes' own fluent five-speed automatic. Yes, the SL500 is automatic only, a transmission that perfectly suits the car. Because it weighs 45kg less (thanks to the alloy body panels) and is more slippery than the SL Mk4, it offers more performance, though the 6.3sec to 62mph, just 0.2sec quicker, doesn't communicate its point-to-point potential, or its sporting personality.

Here, steering and suspension play the crucial role. A quick, 2.6-turn, rack and pinion set-up replaces the old SL's recirculating ball system, cutting more than half a turn from the steering, and replacing the slop around the straight ahead with precision and accuracy. The steering – integrated into the computer-controlled ABC suspension so responses are quicker in Sport mode – is lighter than its predecessor's. At its most direct between 37 and 87mph and quicker around the centre, it's the steering that makes the new SL so

Cabin more spacious; seats superb; rack and pinion steering precise

NEXT EVOLUTION OF NEW SL

The SL500 is only the first of a raft of variants for Mercedes' new sports car.

Already the supercharged 470bhp SL55 AMG – the fastest accelerating production Mercedes-Benz ever – has broken cover. Next year, simultaneously with the SL's March 2002 launch in America, a new 3.5-litre V6 version, with standard steel suspension, brings SL ownership a little closer.

Expect the SL350's near £55,000 price to undercut the SL500 by 10 grand.

The first round of new engines will be completed with the arrival, late next year, of the awesome SL600 V12.

Within the next two years, all Mercedes petrol engines are likely to be converted to direct injection for a further increase in performance and an added 10-15 percent fuel saving.

Mercedes Benz
W230 Series SL500

SUPER ROADSTER
SPECIAL

Suspension firms
up in corners;
roll is minimal

Mercedes Benz
W230 Series SL500

"AT THE END OF A LONG DAY'S DRIVING YOU ONLY WANT TO KEEP GOING AND NEVER GIVE BACK THE KEYS."

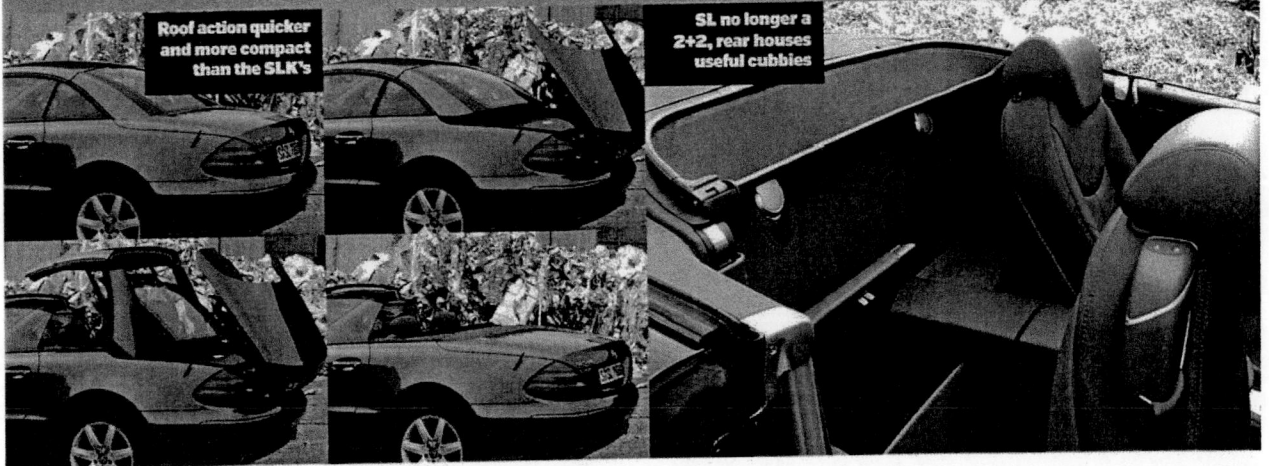

Roof action quicker and more compact than the SLK's

SL no longer a 2+2, rear houses useful cubbies

Mercedes Benz
W230 Series SL500

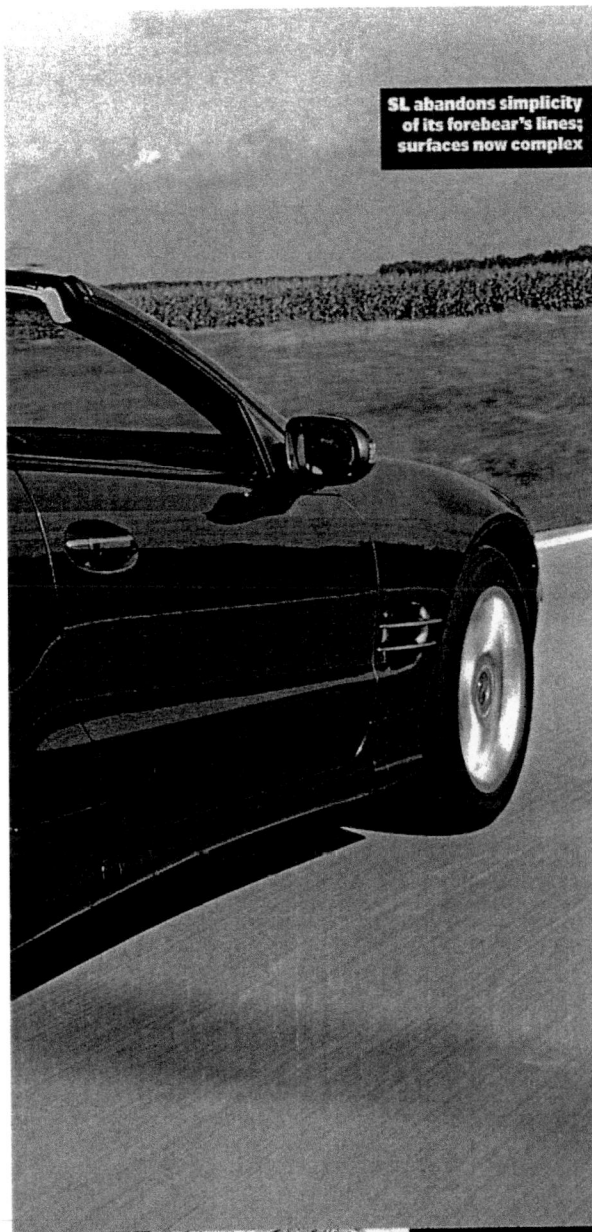

SL abandons simplicity of its forebear's lines; surfaces now complex

302bhp V8 is not a new engine, but it suits SL superbly

fluent. Yet you can separate the steering from the suspension. Cruise on the motorway and, if it wasn't for the distinctive whine of the Michelins, you could be in a lwb S-class limo, so soft and compliant is the ride, isolating the cabin from the road in a most un-sports-car-like manner.

Attack a corner, or switch to Sport, and the suspension firms up, reducing steady state roll angles. Where the previous SL rolled to seven degrees at 37mph through a slalom course, the new SL cuts the roll angles to three degrees in comfort mode and just 2.5 in Sport. At maximum lateral acceleration the difference stretches from the Mk4 SL's 4.1 degrees to 0.9 degrees.

If advanced technology is to work, it must bring benefits without the driver or occupants being conscious of anything unusual. That is why the SL is so impressive. When the ride needs to firm up it does, without the driver being aware of the change-over. The SL then sweeps through fast corners and hairpins with the same effortlessness and the mildest of understeer. It's fluent, fast and easy.

You can't disengage Mercedes' stability control (ESP), but you can delay the onset of electronic intervention to an extent few SL owners will ever approach. Set-up thus, you can balance the car's attitude on the throttle. Mostly it feels remarkably wieldy, but the SL still weighs 1770kg, and there are moments – when you need to change direction from one lock and back again – when the constraints of a heavy two-seater become apparent. The suspension plays a key role in helping the body (torsional rigidity is up 20 percent) to feel remarkably taut – there's no steering column shake or scuttle movement.

Likewise the electronic brakes. They're progressive and immensely powerful, and Mercedes' long pedal travel has been shortened. But they're still steel brakes; the ceramic system, introduced on the CL 55 AMG last year, isn't even an option.

Looking on as photographer Stan Papior does his stuff, I take the time to soak up the SL's styling, the work of Steve Mattin, the Brit who styled the A-class. The beautifully tapered front is the most successful angle, yet another evolution of Mercedes' current merged circular headlight theme with a large three-pointed star dominating the traditional SL-shaped grille. The two vents just forward of the windscreen, each with three longitudinal alloy strakes, seem unnecessarily forced, however.

In profile, roof down, you're struck by two things: the contrived nature of the pretend vent behind the front wheel-arch – an SL design cue Mercedes isn't prepared to discard – and the droopy tail. To my eyes, the SL is more handsome as a coupé. The simplicity of the previous SL has been replaced by more complex, vaguely strained, shapes and surfaces, and there's an excess of crease lines. I've no doubt most SL customers will love it.

In short, it's the driving experience that shows the SL off to greatest advantage. No car – and this has been true of the SL for four generations – is better able to shrug off the normal compromises of a sports car, and play the hedonist equally well. More SL driving time please. ●

SUPER ROADSTER SPECIAL

Factfile

MERCEDES-BENZ SL500

How much?	
Price	£68,640 (est)
On sale in UK	April 2002
How fast?	
0-60mph	6.3sec
Top speed	155mph
How thirsty?	
Urban	14.8mpg
Extra urban	30.7mpg
Combined mpg	22.2mpg
How big?	
Length	4535mm
Width	1815mm
Height	1298mm
Wheelbase	2560mm
Weight	1770kg
Fuel tank	80 litres

Engine
Layout 8 cyls in vee, 4966cc
Max power 302bhp at 5600rpm
Max torque 339lb ft from 2700-4200rpm
Specific output 61bhp per litre
Power to weight 171bhp per tonne
Installation Longitudinal, front, rear-wheel drive
Bore/stroke 97.0/84.0mm
Made of Alloy head and block
Compression ratio 10.0:1
Valve gear 3 valves per cylinder, sohc
Ignition and fuel Microprocessor controlled ignition and injection

Gearbox
Type Five-speed automatic
Ratios/mph per 1000rpm
1st 3.60/7.6 **2nd** 2.19/12.5
3rd 1.41/19.5 **4th** 1.00/27.5
5th 0.83/33.1
Final drive 2.82

Suspension
Front and rear Multi-link, coil springs and Active Body Control
Rear Independent multi-link, coil springs, Active Body Control

Steering
Type Rack and pinion, power assisted
Lock to lock 2.6

Brakes
Front 330mm ventilated, cross-drilled discs
Rear 300mm ventilated discs

Wheels and tyres
Size 8Jx17in
Made of Alloy
Tyres 255/45 ZR17 Michelin Pilot Sport
All figures are manufacturer's claims

Verdict

The luxury two-seater than can instantly transform itself into a proper sports car. Remarkable refinement and comfort

Mercedes Benz
W230 Series SL500

MERCEDES
SL 500

Mercedes hopes to assert its dominance yet again in the supercoupé/roadster market with the latest version of the monumental SL. But has it upped the stakes enough?

Mercedes Benz
W230 Series SL500

AUTOCAR
ROAD TEST
Number 4520

MERCEDES-BENZ
Model tested SL 500
List price £68,500 (est)
Top speed 155mph
30-70mph 5.2sec
0-60mph 5.8sec
60-0mph 2.4sec
MPG 18.7

For Styling, performance, roof, chassis, desirability
Against Trim quality, some steering kickback

Only once in the past 20 years has anything rivalled the Mercedes SL's status as the world's greatest all-rounder. There was little cause for concern at Stuttgart though, because however gripping I.T. Botham's 1981 Ashes series might have been, he was never going to affect sales of the most versatile sports car in history. Even now they don't know what cricket is.

The SL had few rivals. Not surprising for a car that nailed the needs of its owners so successfully. Sure, the Jaguar XK8 and Porsche 911 got close, but in reality no other manufacturer had the balls to ask the SL to step outside. It had too much image.

Now there's a new version. Project R230 began in 1996, and the brief was obvious: take the current car's abilities and move all the adjectives into the comparative form. It seems to have worked: faster, lighter, roomier and more desirable than ever, the new SL is proof the hybrid supercoupé/roadster market belongs to Merc.

This is a case helped enormously by a costly but competitive list price. At a predicted £68,500, the SL 500 tested here could finally be the perfect all-trader.

DESIGN & ENGINEERING

Some key information for those thinking the SL is going to be a hardcore sports car, or live up to its SL name (Sports Light): it weighs a staggering 400kg more than a

HISTORY The first SL or 'Sports Light' appeared in 1954. The 300SL Gullwing is one of the most desirable Mercs ever, and set in motion a series of models that had geriatric lifespans: 19 years for the Mk2, that found fame as the JR Ewing runaround, and 12 years for the last-generation Mk3. Highlights include the 7.3-litre SL73, the charming, original 500SL of the early '80s and, of course, the original Gullwing. Best forgotten is the SLC: a stretched 2+2 that looked awkward and was a motor sport flop.

Porsche 996, comes as an automatic only and will eventually sit beneath the SLR supercar in the family tree. Looks more tourer than sportster, then.

As does the engine spec. No high revving, small capacity motor here. Just three valves per cylinder and a 6000rpm red line are all that's needed. From 4996cc it produces 310bhp at 5600rpm and 339lb ft of torque from 2700-4200rpm.

It looks like just another unstressed big V8 on the surface, but this is a thoroughly modern drive-train that incorporates a five-speed automatic 'box with the ability to adjust to different driving styles and meet EU4 emissions regulations. It's very clean indeed. But despite the big numbers and promise of more than ample performance, it's the rest of the SL's innards that showcase what Merc is capable of.

This is the first road-car application of the company's new Sensotronic Brake control system (SBS). A new electro-hydraulic system (brake-by-wire to most of us) means the left pedal is no longer in direct fluid contact with the caliper pistons. Five years of development has creat-

> ## "The brief was obvious – make it faster, lighter, roomier and even more desirable"

ed a four-disc set-up whose pedal actuation is linked electronically to an ECU with brake force distributed to each wheel according to the demands registered by the pedal.

Beyond the obvious weight saving (no brake booster under the bonnet), SBS offers performance advantages. Data can be used from the stability control and active suspension systems to calculate stopping power and, more impressively, SBS calculates the force for each wheel. So it may be a touch heavy, but the braking should be more than up to the task.

Next on the SL's sci-fi spec list is the Active Body Control suspension system, a modified version of the set-up first seen on the CL Coupé two years ago. It mixes a conventional spring and damper at each corner with a hydraulically controlled servo cylinder that manages body roll for the best ride and handling compromise.

But the roof is still the SL's party piece. This time it's a retractable hard-top that goes by the name of vario-roof. No less than 17 motors help carry out contortion acts like spinning the rear screen through 180deg to give more boot space when it's stowed. It's a balletic display of robotics and takes just 16sec to go up or down.

GREAT STYLING MEETS GROUND-BREAKING TECH ★★★★★

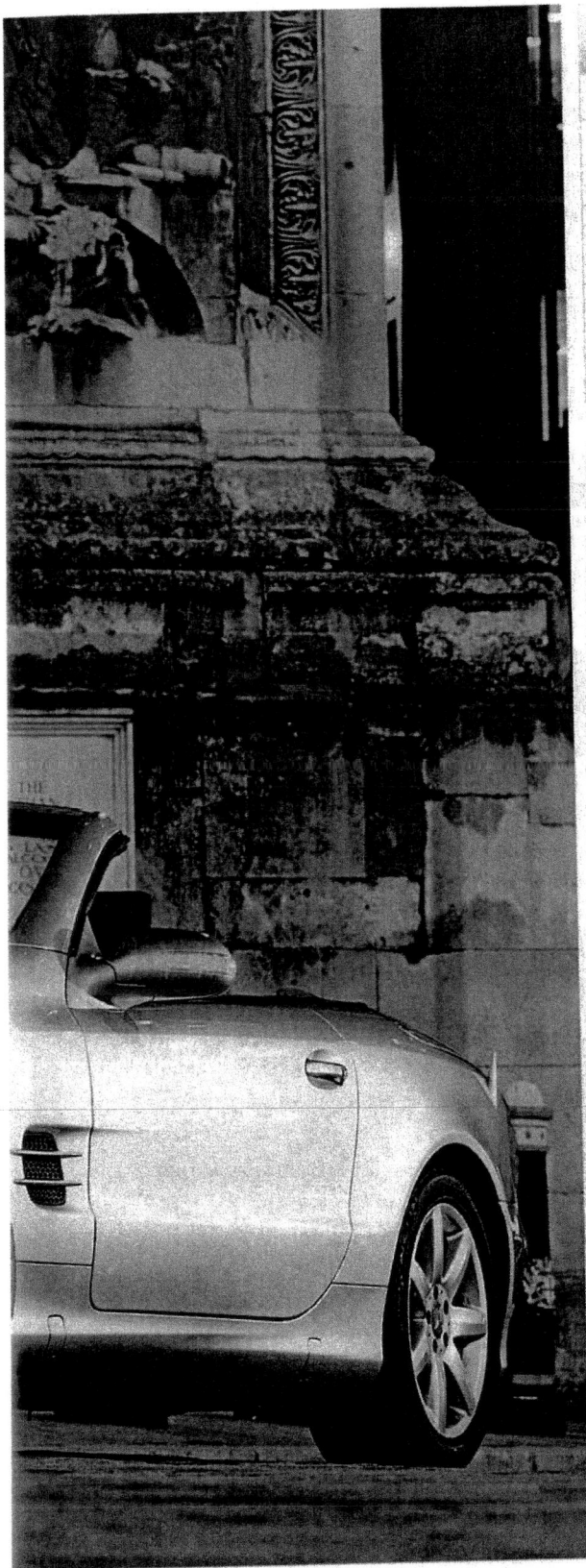

ROAD TEST MERCEDES-BENZ SL 500

PERFORMANCE & BRAKES

This is more like it: no paddles and no buttons. The SL has a real automatic gearbox, one made by the world's pre-eminent specialist in the subject. A 'box whose ability to mix the disciplines of chilled layabout and quick-shifter make it a pleasure to use. And a key part of the SL's rare depth of character.

On to the test track. Select D for Drive, hammer the rather pretty chrome and rubber-faced accelerator into the carpet and watch the needles move. Extracting numbers from an SL is no more dramatic than that. For two reasons: first, straight-line performance as a specialist subject has moved on considerably since the previous-generation car, and the new car is little faster against the clock anyway. And second, with the kind of mechanical refinement the SL offers, it would need to thump both passenger and driver against the headrests to make them realise how accelerative it was.

It's plenty fast enough though. The figures add up to 0-60mph in 5.8sec and 0-100mph in 13.5sec. But the SL is in fact considerably slower than the smaller and cheaper SLK 32 AMG, which somehow manages to hit 100mph in 11.2sec. But as you'll know, there are ways of going about your acceleration, and the SL's is quite addictive. The engine may not have the same big-tech claims as the chassis, but it's a key part of the SL experience. Throttle response is keen at any engine speed and it makes a pleasantly suggestive noise at low speeds. It's docile, refined and a doddle in traffic.

And it revs. Just three valves per cylinder and maximum power coming in at 5600rpm shouldn't be the on-paper credentials of a motor this keen to hammer into its rev limiter. Up the pace, though – all the way to its electronically limited top speed of 155mph – and the engine is more than happy to oblige. The sound is butch enough to make you feel special and refinement is first rate. It loves low engine speeds, too. At 40mph, only a concerted shove on the accelerator will see the Merc shift down a gear: there's enough torque to just go with the flow.

And then there's that gearchange. Quite simply, it's reference-point stuff. Smooth, fast and dynamic enough to adjust to individual driving styles, the change is superb. Even full power shifts aren't noticeable. Better still, the semi-automatic mode is more intuitive – despite working from side to side – than any other we've tested, and will hold on to gears as and when required.

The SL's brakes are brilliant. Their ability to keep the car stable under big loads in bends and apply maximum braking pressure in a split second is remarkable. The SBS system's best trick is allowing the driver a small amount of controllable lock-up in certain situations. Rather than leave the anti-lock system pulsing annoyingly through the pedal, SBS feels like an unassisted system working on the very edge of the available grip.

GOES SLOW AS WELL AS IT GOES FAST. AWESOME BRAKES ★★★★

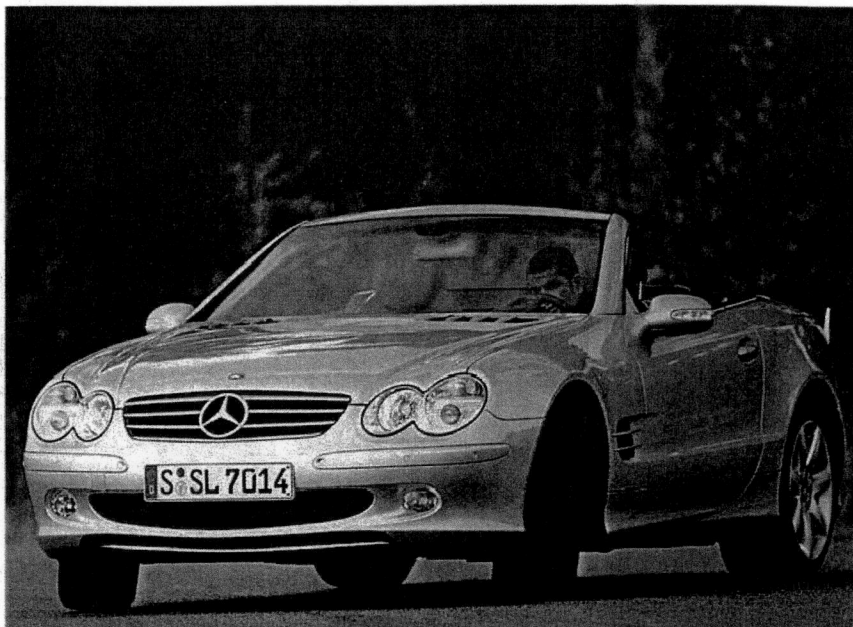
ABC system ensures SL rides well and handles brilliantly: tech just refuses to allow car to roll in corners

Superb auto gearbox and sharp, accurate steering

Roof rotates as it stows to provide more boot space

SL no lightweight sportster; it weighs 400kg more than a Porsche 996

Active suspension provides best compromise of ride and handling

Slippery coupé shape has a drag coefficient of 0.29

Brake-by-wire system distributes brakeforce electronically

SL feels equally at home at low and high speeds; it hits 60mph in 5.8sec and tops out at a limited 155mph

Mercedes Benz
W230 Series SL500

Performance and specifications

Engine
Layout 8 cyls in vee, 4996cc
Max power 310bhp at 5600rpm
Max torque 339lb ft from 2700-4200rpm
Power to weight 168bhp per tonne
Torque to weight 184lb ft per tonne
Specific output 62bhp per litre
Installation Front, longitudinal, rear-wheel drive
Construction Alloy head and block
Bore/stroke 97/84mm
Valve gear 3 valves per cylinder, dohc per bank
Compression ratio 10.0:1
Ignition and fuel HFM fuel injection and engine management

Gearbox
Type 5-speed automatic with touchshift
Ratios/mph per 1000rpm
1st 3.60/7.6 **2nd** 2.19/12.5
3rd 1.41/19.5 **4th** 1.00/27.5
5th 0.83/33.1
Final drive 2.82

Maximum speeds
5th 155mph/4680rpm **4th** 155/5640
3rd 117/6000 **2nd** 75/6000
1st 46/6000

Acceleration from rest
Surface dry

True mph	sec	speedo mph
30	2.3	31
40	3.2	41
50	4.4	52
60	5.8	62
70	7.5	72
80	9.4	83
90	11.3	93
100	13.5	103

Standing qtr mile 14.4sec/99mph
Standing km 26.0sec/129mph
30-70mph through gears 5.2sec

Acceleration in kickdown

mph	sec	gear
20-40	1.9	1
30-50	2.1	1/2
40-60	2.6	1/2
50-70	3.1	2
60-80	3.6	2/3
70-90	3.8	3
80-100	4.1	3

Steering
Type Rack and pinion, power assisted
Turns lock to lock 2.6

Layout
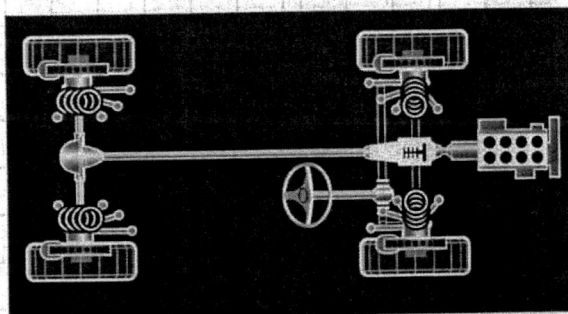

Suspension
Front Multi-link, coil springs, active body control
Rear Multi-link, coil springs, active body control

Wheels & tyres
Wheels 8Jx17in
Made of Cast alloy
Tyres 255/45 ZR17 Michelin Pilot Sport
Spare Emergency puncture kit

Brakes
Front 330mm ventilated cross-drilled discs
Rear 300mm ventilated cross-drilled discs
Anti-lock Standard

Gearing
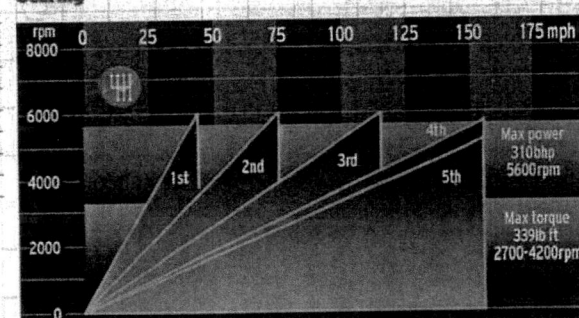

Body 2-door roadster **Cd** 0.29 **Front/rear tracks** 1559/1547mm
Turning circle 11.02m **Min/max front leg room** 880/1140mm
Min/max front head room 820/910mm **Interior width** 1400mm
Boot width 1300mm **Boot length** 670mm **Max boot height** 460mm
Kerb weight 1840kg **Width (inc mirrors)** 2045mm

bp — All Autocar road tests are conducted using BP Cleaner Unleaded Fuel or BP Cleaner Diesel with additives to help keep engines cleaner

Brakes
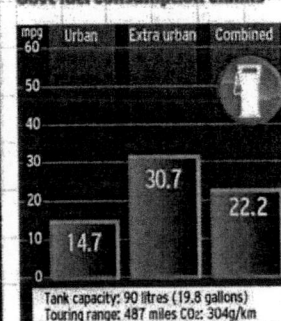
60-0mph: 2.5sec

m	30 mph	50 mph	70 mph	st qtr mile
	8.9	24.1	46.6	96.2 99mph

SURFACE DRY

Fuel consumption test results
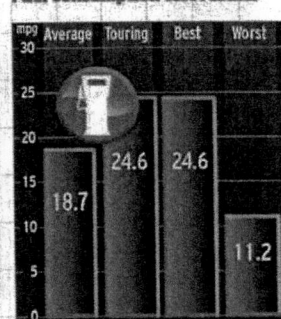

mpg	Average	Touring	Best	Worst
	18.7	24.6	24.6	11.2

Govt fuel consumption claims
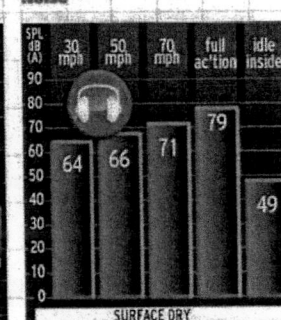

mpg	Urban	Extra urban	Combined
	14.7	30.7	22.2

Tank capacity: 90 litres (19.8 gallons)
Touring range: 487 miles CO₂: 304g/km

Noise

SPL dB(A)	30 mph	50 mph	70 mph	full ac'tion	idle inside
	64	66	71	79	49

SURFACE DRY

AUTOCAR ROAD TESTS
....are the most exhaustive published in the UK. Each car is measured in detail, then performance, speed and brake tested on a neutral proving ground. We also try to cover at least 500 miles on all types of road, and measure economy in all conditions.

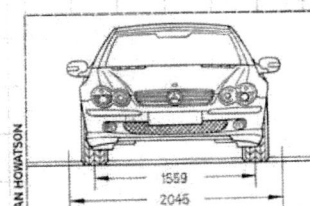

1559
2045

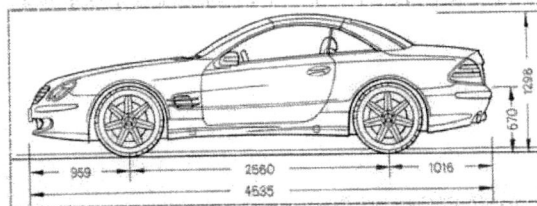

959   2560   1016
4535
670   1298

IAN HOWATSON

The performance figures were taken with the odometer reading 1700 miles. **AUTOCAR** test results are protected by world copyright and may not be reproduced without the editor's written permission

Mercedes Benz
W230 Series SL500

HANDLING & RIDE

This is the area where the SL's intended duality of character must have caused Mercedes engineers the biggest difficulties. Here is a car that needs to be comfortable but agile, stable but responsive, and above all safe. It's trying to perfect an art that the world's best chassis alchemists have been trying for decades, namely: to make a car that rides and really handles.

The SL gets agonisingly close to perfection in most areas and proves that Merc's decision to develop a hybrid suspension system comprising active and conventional components was spot on.

Crawling round town, the ride quality is excellent. Not the kind that will get S-class drivers jealous, but well beyond anything a 996 driver will have experienced. Small, aggravating intrusions just get swept up by the dampers and the bodyshell doesn't flex or shimmy.

Up the speed a little and the SL's ride is at its very best. A steady cruise is meat 'n' drink to this car: all body movements in check, relying on that structural rigidity to allow spring, damper and active hydraulics to do their stuff. Even big exec saloons won't offer much more comfort.

And then you get to the road you've been waiting for. No need to select the sport button to firm things up: the SL spots that you want to go fast and firms things up for you. It's a useful touch, because you'll be too busy trying to work out how on earth the car does what it does. Body control is the first thing you notice. So adept are the car's active hydraulics at dealing with all the road can throw at you, it is almost disconcerting just how much speed you can carry. Up to a point, and for the first time in our experience, this is a chassis that only allows the speedo needle and wind noise to tell the driver how fast he's going.

It's fun too: agile in a way that something the chubby side of 1800kg has no right to be. A quick 2.6 turns between locks gives the steering precision and accuracy. This is a car that can be aimed confidently down a road, rather than steered defensively in reaction to its size.

But it still isn't a true sports car. Weight transfers eventually build to an uncomfortable level, and despite doing a great job of containing body roll, the active suspension keeps the front end so stiff that the steering can kick back sharply over mid-corner bumps.

Despite that, it's a groundbreaking chassis that will satisfy the needs of nearly every prospective buyer perfectly.

TECHNOLOGY TURNED PERFECTLY INTO ON-ROAD ABILITY ★★★★★

COMFORT SAFETY & EQUIPMENT

Nothing else with two doors and a removable roof can match the comfort levels the SL offers. Much of what it achieves is attributable to the previous section of this test – that ride quality in particular – but

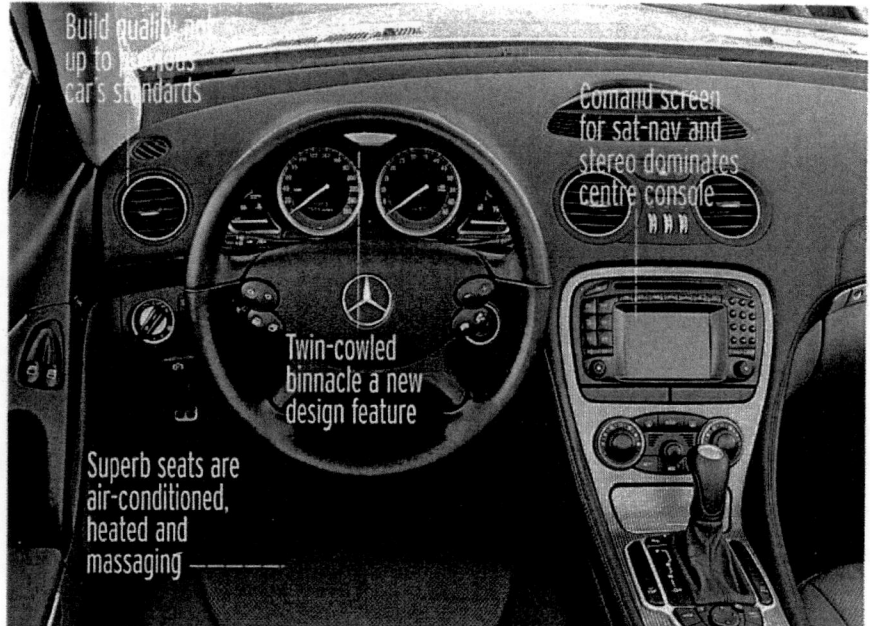

Build quality not up to previous car's standards

Comand screen for sat-nav and stereo dominates centre console

Twin-cowled binnacle a new design feature

Superb seats are air-conditioned, heated and massaging

Plenty of neat design touches inside but trim quality can't match that of its rock solid predecessor

Interior feels quiet and comfy even with the roof down

V8 develops 310bhp and meets stringent emissions regs

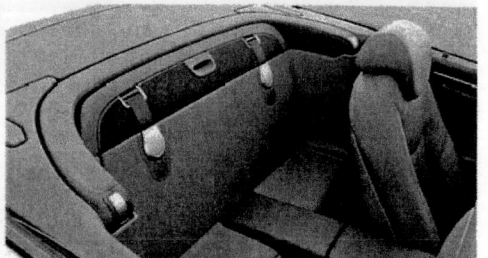

Vario-roof hard-top folds down electronically in just 16sec; decent space in rear even with roof stowed

Mercedes Benz
W230 Series SL500

the cabin is equally important.

Roof up or down, there's ample space for both occupants. Seat technology at DaimlerChrysler has got a bit silly, and the heated, air-conditioned, massaging, electric sports seats prove that the chair fetishists are still catered for. They're fabulously supportive and comfortable and every one of those gimmicks is a bonus.

Twin cowled instruments are the most distinctive feature of a dash that shows how hard the company is trying to reinvent itself. Ergonomically it works well. The instruments are clearly marked in a distinctly un-Merc typeface and the regular Comand sat-nav/communications monitor dominates the centre console.

But the material and build quality just isn't in the same league as the old car. Trim feels lighter and flimsier and the switchgear itself just isn't as sturdy as you'd expect from this marque. Yes, the SL's cabin flatters you with some very neat design touches, but as with every other recent Mercedes, the cost-cutting campaign is noticeable inside.

Luckily, the Merc's schizophrenic character more than makes up for it. In coupé mode, it's as cosy as you'd ever want. Wind noise isn't an issue at motorway speeds, but push beyond three figures and it's quite obvious that the roof

Smart alloy wheels are 17-inchers

isn't fixed in place, despite the 0.29 drag coefficient.

Top down it's very impressive. You'll need the manually fixed wind deflector for perfect results, but the SL is so refined when topless that you find yourself getting impatient for the whole 16 seconds it takes to stow the roof, so long as it's not raining.

The mechanism itself is real performance art, but there are practical reasons for the screen being turned upside down when stowed – it means more boot space. There's even a button that moves the roof up a foot when it's stowed, to make access to the boot easier. Attention to detail is, once again, one of the SL's strongest assets, and one that will make it devastatingly desirable in the showroom.

Active and passive safety levels are incredible. All the electric chassis aids make it easier to avoid a prang in the first place, but two-stage activation for the twin front and side airbags, the obligatory SL pop-up roll bar, and some clever bodyshell and panel construction could make it the best ever contestant in Euro NCAP's crash tests. Not bad for a sports car.

ALMOST UNBEATABLE IN EVERY AREA ★★★★☆

ECONOMY

Weight and power take their toll on the SL. Admittedly, the test car was given a fairly hard time, but we still couldn't average anything more than 18.7mpg and that figure plummeted to a horrendous 11.2mpg at the test track.

At least the 90-litre fuel tank gives a decent touring range, even when there's a heavy right foot involved. For the record, on our touring route the SL recorded 24.6mpg, still a lower figure than we would have expected – but on reflection not bad for a 5.0-litre V8.

NO HIDING FROM THE BIG V8'S THIRST ★★★

MARKET & FINANCE

Given the recent cut in interest rates, ploughing money into an SL might just be wiser than a trip to the building society. Demand for this car is predictably strong and no-one understands the intricacies of supply and strong residuals better than Mercedes-Benz.

Brilliant engineering and comprehensive three-year/60,000-mile warranty cover make the whole proposition even more attractive.

Only the threat of closure for some franchised Mercedes dealerships and build quality that is no longer the envy of the motor industry could damage the ownership proposition.

SO GOOD IT SHOULD BE SOLD BY BUILDING SOCIETIES ★★★★☆

What it costs

On-the-road price	£68,500 (est)
Total as tested	£68,500 (est)
Cost per mile	na
CO₂	304g/km

Equipment
(**bold** = options fitted to test car)

Air-conditioning	●
Traction/stability control	●
Leather trim	●
Electric front seats	●
Sat-nav	●
RDS stereo/CD player	●
Height/tilt-adjust steering	●/●
Anti-lock brakes	●
Airbag driver/passenger/side	●/●/●
Alarm/immobiliser	●/●
Metallic paint	●

● standard

Insurance group	20
Typical quote	£1669

Warranty
3 years/60,000 miles

Servicing
Computer controlled

Part prices

Oil filter	na
Air filter	na
Brake pads f/r	na
Exhaust	na
Door mirror	na
Tyre f/r	£127.00
Windscreen	na
Headlamp unit	na
Front wing	na

THE AUTOCAR VERDICT

THE SHEER APPEAL of the new SL is extraordinary. It has so much to offer to so many people that it's impossible not to hail it as one of the most complete sports cars ever built. But, thankfully for the opposition, it isn't absolutely flawless. Grabbed by the scruff of the neck it does an admirable job of hiding its weight, but given the amount of aluminium used its kerb weight is still fairly high. And those interior trim and build gripes that are beginning to sound like regular *Autocar* moans, detract from the car's appeal. However attractive the cabin may be, it doesn't give the same confidence as the old car that it'll be as durable. But there's enough engineering quality to make you forget this very quickly. The SL is a rare treat: a German car whose technology doesn't intimidate, but adds to its personality.

TESTERS' NOTES

That pop-up roll bar is still too eager to show itself in public. Uneven ground or a little oversteer will set it off. At least it's easily restowed

No bulbs in your SL indicators. LEDs light up faster and brighter, so they're used instead

Don't press the air suspension button if you want to look cool: it raises the car up a good 30mm

Amazing how dated the SLK suddenly looks. Parked next to this car it's stumpy and too upright

Inspired roadster, great coupé ★★★★★

The small print © Autocar 2001. Further information on the SL 500 contact DaimlerChrysler UK Ltd, Tongwell, Milton Keynes MK15 8BA (tel 01908 245000; www.daimlerchrysler.co.uk). The cost-per-mile figure is calculated over three years/36,000 miles and includes depreciation, maintenance, road tax, funding and fuel, but not insurance. Figure supplied by Fleet Management Services (01743 261121). The insurance quote is for a 35-year-old professional male with a clean licence and full no-claims bonus, living in Swindon, supplied by What Car? Insurance. Contract hire figure is based on a lease for three years/36,000 miles, includes maintenance and is supplied by British Car Contracts (0870 902 3311).

79

Mercedes-Benz SL65

Mercedes' in-house team takes on the SLR with a bespoke SL

MODEL TESTED **SL65 Black Series**

● **Price** £249,500 ● **Power** 661bhp ● **Torque** 737lb ft ● **0-60mph** 4.2sec
● **Fuel economy** 15.8mpg ● **CO_2 emissions** 344g/km ● **70-0mph** 42.8m ● **Skidpan** 1.06g

This is only the third Black Series model from Mercedes-Benz's AMG high-performance subsidiary and, if the first two are anything to go by, it could go either way. The first Black Series model, based on the SLK, was so dynamically comical that it would struggle to outpoint a hot hatch. The CLK, on the other hand, was brilliant.

Which brings us to the SL65 Black Series. Like the SLK (and this is crucial to the Black Series ethos), it now has a fixed roof rather than the folding top of the regular SL. Black Series cars are

WE LIKE Effortless performance ● High grip levels ● Fine chassis balance

1 Black-painted wheels fill their arches impressively (limited suspension travel allows that more easily); they're 19 inches in diameter front and 20s at the rear.

2 Front wings are no less than 14cm wider than the standard items and now sit very proud of the doors, the one part of the car whose profile is (partly) unchanged.

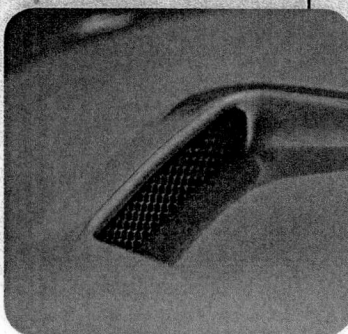

3 Bonnet is lighter than standard (because of carbonfibre construction) but still gets gas struts to lift it. Big vents have one purpose: to remove hot air from the engine bay.

4 Low, protruding and eminently whackable, the front splitter is carbonfibre, which makes it expensive to make and repair or replace.

intended to be stiffer and lighter, and that rules out stowing roofs.

Carbonfibre, meanwhile, abounds on the Black Series SL's bodywork – including the construction of its new fixed roof and massive wheel arch extensions – while the car sports a modified version of the regular SL65's twin-turbo 6.0-litre V12, which usually totes 604bhp. Here it has no less than 661bhp, which puts it on the list of the 10 most powerful production cars in history. As with the SLK and CLK, the Black Series SL carries a premium over the regular SL65, pushing its price to a very serious £249,500.

DESIGN AND ENGINEERING
★★★★☆

Powerful the SL65 Black Series may be, but look for something bespoke in the 5980cc V12 engine and you'll find nothing more than new induction and exhaust systems and the fact that it wears bigger turbochargers than the standard SL65's engine.

There are no internal mechanical changes to the unit, which has so much latent potential that its 661bhp is developed at an easy 5400rpm, →

HISTORY
Although recent SLs are associated with open-topped comfort, the original gullwing 300SL was a supercar of its day. But it wasn't until several generations later, with the R129, that Mercedes first dropped a V12 into an SL, with the 389bhp SL600. AMG produced the rare 7.3-litre SL73 and the rarer still SL70. With the current generation came the twin-turbo 6.0-litre SL65. The Black Series SLK55 appeared in 2006, followed in 2007 by the CLK63.

SL73's V12 developed 525bhp (the SL70 made 496bhp)

WE DON'T LIKE Boosty power delivery ● Gearbox not suited to track driving ● Firm ride

5 The rear spoiler is carbonfibre too and extends by 12cm above 75mph. Subtle it isn't, and its mechanism robs a lot of boot space. You can even raise it manually for cleaning.

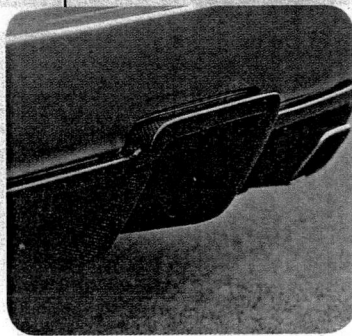

6 Diffuser is made of carbonfibre (who'd have thought?), but as well as its lift-reducing properties, airflow through it also cools the limited-slip differential.

7 Carbonfibre roof has an integral roll bar and, because it doesn't fold, is allowed a flatter profile than regular SLs, plus a larger, more raked rear window for better aerodynamics.

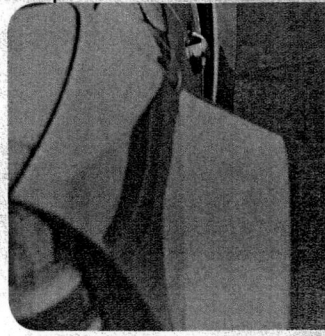

8 Threading a car through tight gap if you've missed with the mirrors you've missed with everything. Don' be quite so confident when driving an SL65 Black, whose rear arches are almost as wide as its mirrors.

Inside out

0.37

880mm min
970mm max

910mm min
1190mm max

260-392 litres

1310mm

980mm   2560mm   1049mm

53%   47%

4589mm

Turning circle: 13.5m

1648mm   1658mm   1960mm

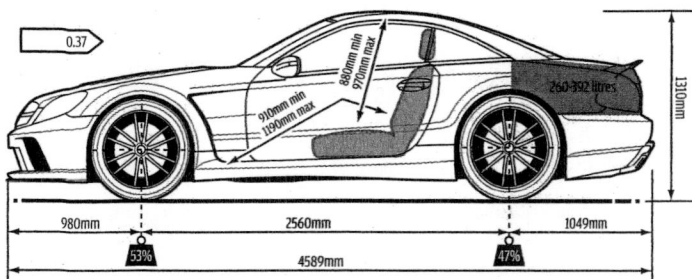

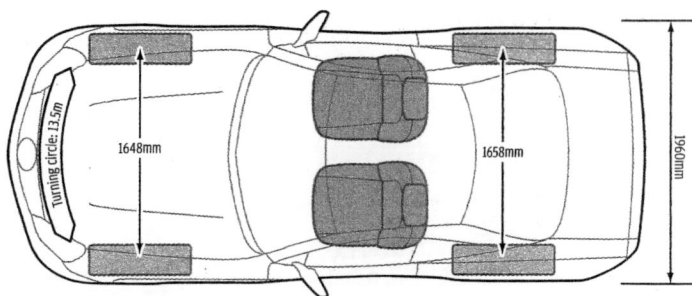

VISIBILITY TEST

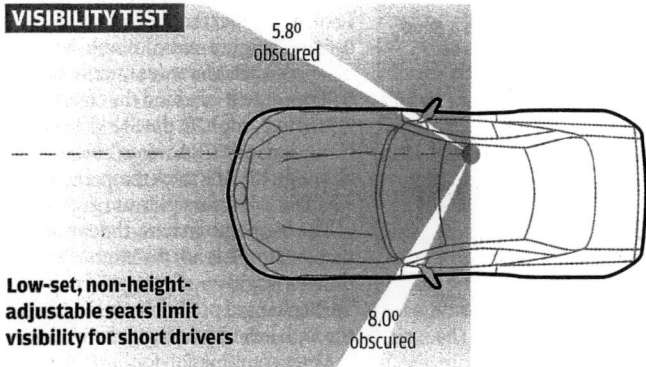

5.8º obscured

Low-set, non-height-adjustable seats limit visibility for short drivers

8.0º obscured

It's dark in here, but the seats are superb and it's easy to get comfortable

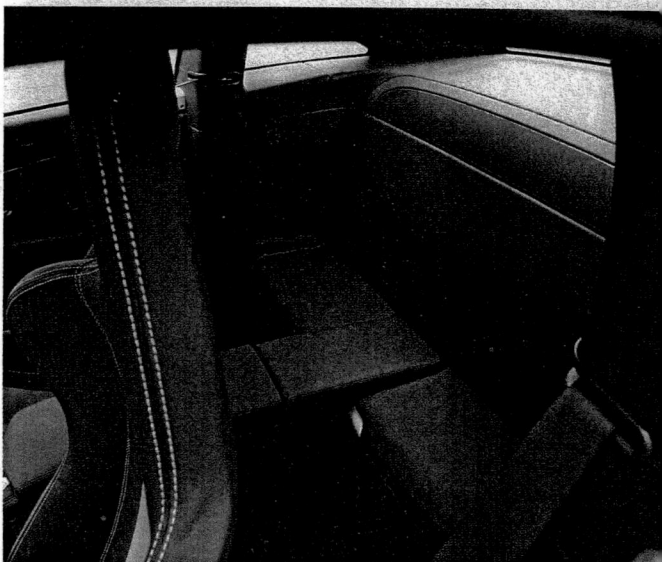

Deep rear bins are useful, and there's room for a couple of squashy bags o

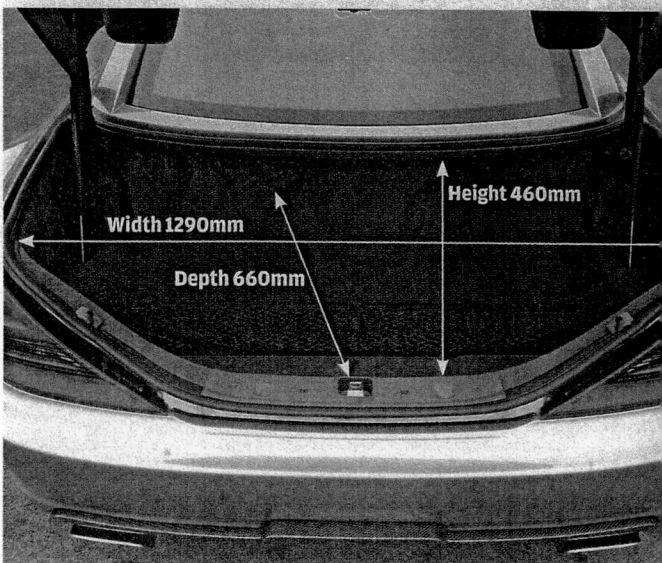

Height 460mm

Width 1290mm

Depth 660mm

With no folding roof, the boot is a decent size, although pop-up wing intrud

← while its torque is electronically limited to 737lb ft between 2200 and 4200rpm. Unlimited, it would generate 885lb ft, sufficient to ruin any transmission Mercedes could conceivably fit to it. As it is, the Black Series retains the SL65's robust five-speed automatic, rather than the seven-speeders of other AMG cars.

However, greater changes abound elsewhere. The SL's steel monocoque is retained but the body, including its reprofiled, fixed roof, is clothed in carbonfibre composites. The Black shares its wheelbase with the regular SL65 but it is slightly longer, lower and – at 1960 versus 1820mm – significantly wider.

With the loss of its metal body panels and roof mechanism, 250kg has been shed; the Black Series' official EC kerb weight is 1870kg. That, however, is still quite a lot for a car which is expected to spend around half of its life on a race track.

To that end, it looks the part; the design of its scoops and flares, aside from their functionality, are meant to emulate AMG's DTM and sportscar racers. Its 97mm wider front and 85mm wider rear track and adjustable suspension (though that's far from the work of a moment) mean it can be set

up to be more (or less) track oriented, too. Ditto the steering system, which has just 1.7 turns lock to lock.

But a conventional five-speed automatic gearbox and steel brakes (carbon-ceramic discs are not an option) are not the general preserve of a track-biased car. Particularly at a quarter of a million pounds.

INTERIOR

★★★½☆

If the SL65 Black's exterior does everything it can to suggest that it is as bespoke as they come, there's little on the inside that screams the same.

The general architecture and feel is lifted straight from the SL65, with the same gearbox, ventilation, stereo and navigation controls. But there are bespoke touches; the door panels, for example, are finished in carbonfibre, and the instrument cluster has been largely redesigned, partly to reflect the fact that this is one Mercedes that might hit 220mph (if it weren't limited to 200mph). The starter button, meanwhile, has moved from its traditional position (in keyless go cars) on top of the gear selector, to occupy the space on the centre →

DRY CIRCUIT
Mercedes SL65 Black
1min 13.0sec
Ferrari 599 GTB
1min 12.7sec

The SL65 is a heavy car, so a 1min 13sec lap time is a quick time. But for all its pace and ability, the SL65 isn't a hugely entertaining track car, the blown powertrain making it difficult to get the most from the chassis.

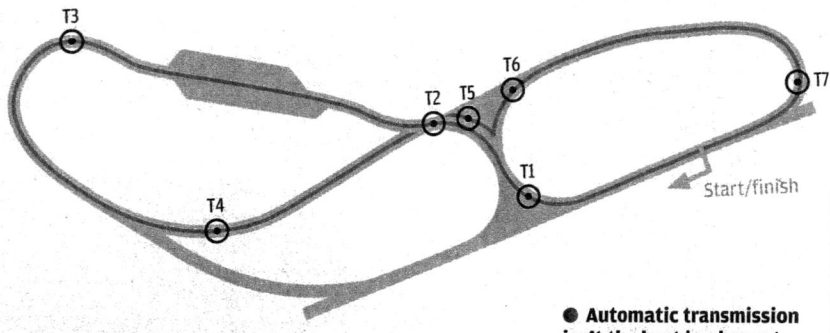

● At the apex of T4, at 110mph, SL65 nudges into understeer. Good steering feedback very welcome.

● Automatic transmission isn't the best implement for finely balancing torque with grip.

WET CIRCUIT
Mercedes SL65 Black
1min 18.6sec
Ferrari 599 GTB
1min 9.9sec

SL65's stiff set-up and abundance of torque cause it problems on the wet circuit. The set-up doesn't make the most of the tyres' ability, and under power the SL easily breaks traction.

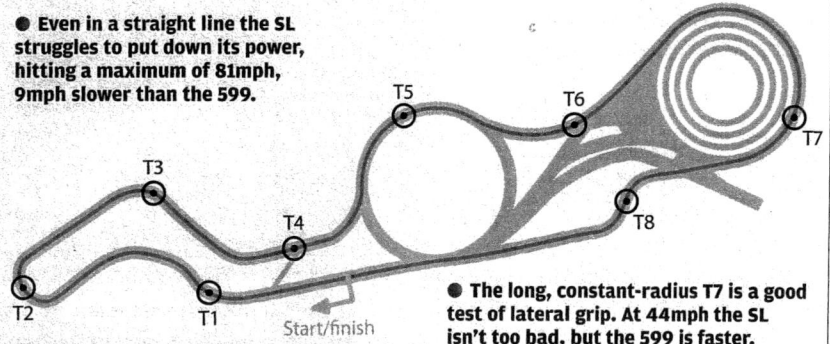

● Even in a straight line the SL struggles to put down its power, hitting a maximum of 81mph, 9mph slower than the 599.

● The long, constant-radius T7 is a good test of lateral grip. At 44mph the SL isn't too bad, but the 599 is faster.

ACCELERATION Dry, clear 9deg C

MB SL65 BLACK Standing quarter 12.3sec at 123.3mph, standing km 21.8sec at 154.5mph, 30-70mph 3.1sec, 30-70mph in 4th 10.4sec

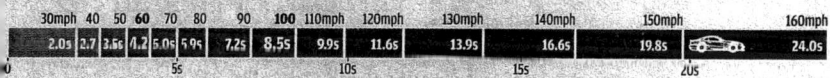

30mph	40	50	60	70	80	90	100	110mph	120mph	130mph	140mph	150mph	160mph
2.0s	2.7	3.6s	4.2s	5.0s	5.9s	7.2s	8.5s	9.9s	11.6s	13.9s	16.6s	19.8s	24.0s

FERRARI 599 Standing quarter 11.7sec at 129.8mph, standing km 20.9sec at 164.6mph, 30-70mph 2.6sec, 30-70mph in 4th 5.8sec

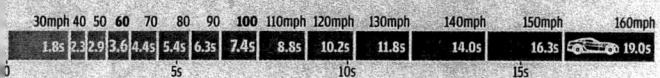

30mph	40	50	60	70	80	90	100	110mph	120mph	130mph	140mph	150mph	160mph
1.8s	2.3	2.9s	3.6	4.4s	5.4s	6.3s	7.4s	8.8s	10.2s	11.8s	14.0s	16.3s	19.0s

BRAKING 60-0mph 2.47sec

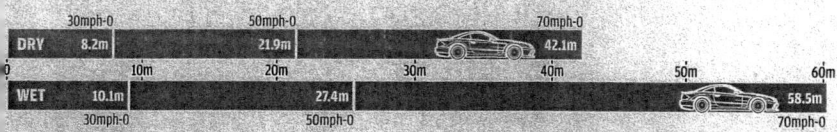

	30mph-0	50mph-0	70mph-0
DRY	8.2m	21.9m	42.1m
WET	10.1m	27.4m	58.5m

← console where the roof controls would usually sit.

Certainly, the SL65's is an interior that befits its Black Series name, because it's as dark inside as they get. The headlining, trim and carpets are all black. So are the seats, which (in European-spec cars) are terrific – carbonfibre-backed and figure-hugging. A couple of our testers found that they gave some lower back ache after a long road drive, but on track they are supportive and suitably adjustable (manually) to an excellent driving position.

Behind the front seats there are the standard storage cubbies, but while the roof's folding mechanism has gone the SL65 Black has gained no greater practicality. While the boot is untroubled by the roof, it is instead filled from the bootlid down by the electrics and mechanics of the spoiler.

PERFORMANCE

★★★★☆

Look no further than the headline 0-60mph figure and you could be disappointed. Mercedes undoubtedly will be: 4.2sec is behind the claimed 3.9sec to 62mph. In the SL's defence, conditions at MIRA weren't ideal; although dry, the track temperature was a little low for optimum grip.

The bigger point here, though, is that 0-60mph is not the interval to do the SL's mighty performance justice. Turbocharged power channelled through an automatic gearbox is not the best combination for finely judged starts. Look instead at the 30-70mph time of 3.1sec, or 80-120mph in 5.7sec. This is a brutally quick car, but also one that, left in its most cosseting mode (transmission in Comfort, ESP on), is also easy to drive. Other than a firm ride and some issues with low-speed manoeuvring, this SL is almost as carefree to drive as any other.

On the Limit

Given the monstrous power going through just the rear wheels, you might well imagine that the SL65 Black is a fearsome machine to drive briskly. While it does demand considerable respect, if the surface is dry and smooth the SL65 is surprisingly docile. There is considerable grip, and traction, due both to the wide tyres (325mm at the rear) and stiff suspension; around the dry handling circuit it generated 1.06g through our measured corner.

Dispense with the three-stage ESP and push harder and what comes first is understeer, although perhaps less than we found on our US first drive

Black Series handles well at speed but its ride is too firm for long journeys

Under the skin

POWER HOUSE

So how deep do the changes over a regular SL65 go? Far, but the Black Series is a heavy modification job, rather than what you might refer to as a model in its own right. Although the carbon panels are all new, the floorpan is taken from the standard car, for example. And the engine? Although none of the internals on this three-valve V12 have changed (like all AMG engines, the unit is still assembled one man), most of the inlet and out ancillaries have. The turbocharger themselves have a 12 per cent large cross-section and the charge air co has had its efficiency improved by per cent. The inlet manifold has be tuned for response and the exhaus modified for a lower back pressure

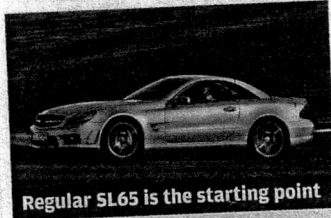

Regular SL65 is the starting point

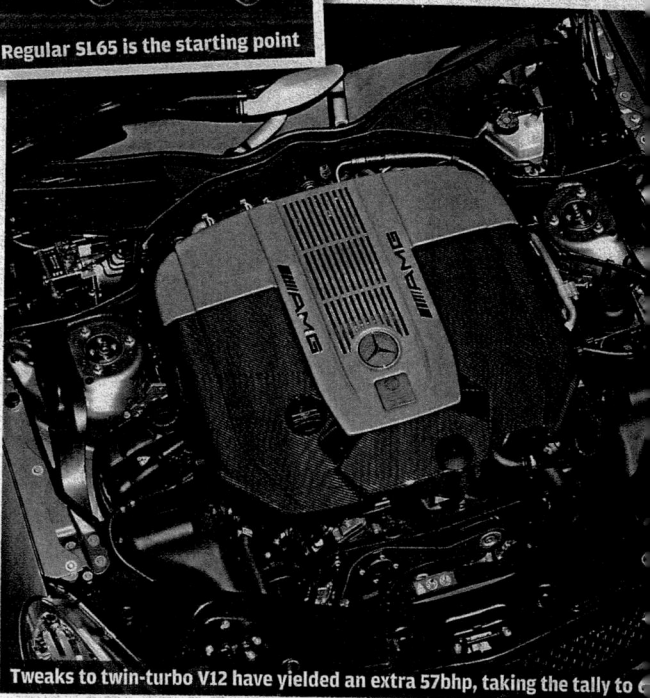

Tweaks to twin-turbo V12 have yielded an extra 57bhp, taking the tally to

Next to gearboxes with eight ratios, the SL's five might sound a little mean, but the reality is that, with such a mountain of torque, more would be overkill. What's more important is that the changes are swift and smooth. Obviously the tyres' grip can easily be overcome if you lean heavily on the throttle, but the ESP's interventions are soft-edged yet incisive.

Truly getting a handle on the engine's capabilities requires selecting the faster of the gearbox's two manual modes and switching to ESP Sport, or dispensing with ESP altogether if you're feeling brave. Although not short on capacity, the blown V12's ramp-up in performance isn't as linear as that of the normally aspirated Ferrari 599. While the 599 builds up to a spine-tingling top end, the Merc has a pronounced mid-range between 2200 and 4200rpm. Accelerate through this zone in the first two gears and the tyres stand little chance as the turbos start to blow.

But it is quick enough to justify the outrageous price tag? While it may seem churlish to question the performance attributes of anything that will hit 100mph in 8.5sec, that it doesn't dip into the elite group of 7.0sec cars is slightly disappointing.

The massive brakes, although not carbon-ceramic, are well judged for road driving, with good bite and pedal modulation. While they stood up reasonably well to our performance tests, with little drop-off in performance over five timed laps, there was considerable heat build-up.

RIDE AND HANDLING

★★★☆☆

With the ability to adjust the ride height, damper and camber settings, there is scope to change the SL65's handling and ride characteristics considerably. If Mercedes' forecast that SL65 Blacks will spend 60 per cent of their time on track proves accurate, this adjustability will be a boon. It does, however, cause us an issue in this road test, as the adjustment is mechanical rather than electric or hydraulic; we can only assess the car as it was delivered to us.

Even in the first few moments there is no mistaking the SL65 for anything but a powerful, rear-wheel-driven car. Manoeuvring at low speeds, the limited-slip differential struggles to cope with full lock (particularly in reverse), sending the inside wheel →

last November (Mercedes can't confirm if the set-up of the two cars differs). For the most part the SL Black commits to corner keenly. Extracting that performance, though, is not quite the enjoyable,

involving process it should be; the car doesn't have the precision needed to accurately balance power with grip through a corner. Which leaves a capable, if not hugely satisfying track car.

Wet conditions are a very different matter. The remains good lateral grip, so corner speeds can b quite high on a constant throttle, but under powe this can disappear in an instant.

Crunching numbers

WHAT IT COSTS

MERCEDES SL65 AMG BLACK SERIES

On-the-road price	£249,500
Price as tested	£249,500
Value after 3yrs/36k miles	na
Contract hire pcm	na
Cost per mile	na
Insurance/typical quote	20/na

EQUIPMENT CHECK LIST

19/20-inch alloy wheels	■
AMG sports steering wheel	■
Anti-theft alarm/immobiliser	■
Carbonfibre bucket seats	■
Carbonfibre door inserts	■
Electric heated door mirrors	■
Front/curtain airbags	■
Cruise control	■
Auto wipers	■
Dual-zone climate control	■
Keyless entry and start	■
Voice-controlled sat-nav	■
CD with MP3 player	■
10-speaker Harmon Kardon surround sound system	■
Television	■
Bluetooth connectivity	■
Metallic paint	■

Options in **bold** fitted to test car
■ = Standard na = not available

RANGE AT A GLANCE

ENGINES	POWER	FROM
6.0 V12	661bhp	£249,500

TRANSMISSION	
5-spd auto	Std

ENGINE

Installation	Front, longitudinal
Type	V12, 5980cc, twin-turbocharged, petrol
Made of	Aluminium block and head
Bore/stroke	82.6mm/93mm
Compression ratio	9.0:1
Valve gear	3 per cyl
Power	661bhp at 5400rpm
Torque	737lb ft at 2200-4200rpm
Red line	6000rpm
Power to weight	353bhp per tonne
Torque to weight	394lb ft per tonne
Specific output	111bhp per litre

POWER & TORQUE

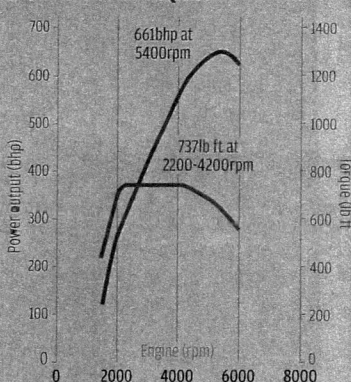

661bhp at 5400rpm
737lb ft at 2200-4200rpm

CHASSIS & BODY

Construction	Steel monocoque
Weight/as tested	1870kg/1880kg
Drag coefficient	0.37
Wheels	19/20in alloy
Tyres	265/35 ZR19 (f), 325/30 ZR20 (r) Dunlop Sport Maxx GT
Spare	Repair kit

TRANSMISSION

Type Rear-wheel drive
Gearbox 5-speed auto
Ratios/mph per 1000rpm
1st 3.6/8.6 **2nd** 2.19/14.2 **3rd** 1.41/22.0
4th 1.0/31.1 **5th** 0.83/37.4
Final drive ratio 2.65

ECONOMY

TEST	Average	15.8mpg
	Touring	22.1mpg
	Track	9.5mpg
CLAIMED	Urban	12.8mpg
	Extra-urban	28.2mpg
	Combined	19.6mpg
	Tank size	80 litres
	Test range	278 miles

SUSPENSION

Front Double wishbones, coil springs, fully adjustable dampers, anti-roll bar
Rear Multi-link, coil springs, fully adjustable dampers, anti-roll bar

STEERING

Type Power-assisted rack and pinion
Turns lock to lock 1.7
Turning circle 13.5m

BRAKES

Front 390mm ventilated discs with six-piston calipers
Rear 360mm ventilated discs with four-piston calipers
Anti-lock Standard, EBD, BA

CABIN NOISE

Idle 49dB **Max revs in third gear** 84dB
30mph 65dB **50mph** 70dB **70mph** 73dB

SAFETY

ABS, EBD, BAS, ESP
EuroNCAP crash rating na
Pedestrian rating na

GREEN RATING

CO_2 emissions 344g/km
Tax at 20/40% pcm na

ACCELERATION

MPH	TIME (sec)
0-30	2.0
0-40	2.7
0-50	3.5
0-60	4.2
0-70	5.0
0-80	5.9
0-90	7.2
0-100	8.5
0-110	9.9
0-120	11.6
0-130	13.9
0-140	16.6
0-150	19.8
0-160	24.0

ACCELERATION IN GEAR

MPH	2nd	3rd	4th	5th
20-40	1.8	-	-	-
30-50	1.5	3.1	6.5	9.1
40-60	1.4	2.4	4.8	7.6
50-70	1.5	2.2	4.0	6.0
60-80	1.6	2.2	3.3	5.2
70-90	-	2.2	3.2	4.5
80-100	-	2.4	3.7	4.3
90-110	-	2.6	4.2	4.6
100-120	-	3.0	4.2	4.9
110-130	-	-	4.2	5.4
120-140	-	-	4.9	6.1
130-150	-	-	5.8	-
140-160	-	-	7.3	-

MAX SPEEDS IN GEAR

1. 52mph 6000rpm
2. 85mph 6000rpm
3. 132mph 6000rpm
4. 186mph 6000rpm
5. 200mph 5347rpm

RPM in 5th @ 70/80mph = 1870/2238

THE SMALL PRINT *Power and torque-to-weight figures are calculated using manufacturer's claimed kerb weight. © Autocar 2009. Test results may not be reproduced without editor's written permission. For information on the SL65 Black Series contact Mercedes-Benz UK Ltd, Tongwell, Milton Keynes, Buckinghamshire, MK15 8BA (00800 1777 7777, www.mercedes-benz.co.uk). Cost-per-mile figures calculated over three years/36,000 miles, including depreciation and maintenance but not insurance; Lloyds TSB Autolease (0870 600 6333). Insurance quote covers 35-year-old professional male with clean licence and full no-claims bonus living in Swindon; from What Car? Insurance (0845 23 2618). Contract hire figure based on a three-year lease/36,000-mile contract including maintenance; from Lombard (0870 902 3311).

AUTOCAR ROAD TEST
Read all of our road tests
autocar.co.uk

← scrabbling. Squeeze the throttle too keenly on the way out of a junction and the SL is very keen to kick sideways as it squats down. Which doesn't exactly bode well for what it might be like exiting a medium-speed corner, but the reality is that with speed and some forces working through it, the suspension ups its game considerably.

Our car had a fraction of understeer dialled in; even in moderate road driving we found ourselves turning into a corner and then adding a fraction more lock. This is most likely a precautionary measure by Mercedes to aid stability, as is the slightly gloopy resistance to the steering away from the straight-ahead. On lock and under load the steering is more communicative and accurate.

Which brings us to the ride quality, which, in the case of our particular example, has to be the SL65 Black's single biggest flaw. There is clearly considerable sophistication to the suspension, which does an admirable job over challenging roads to keep the car level, but there's no hiding from the fact that the ride is very firm. Such that you wouldn't want to cover big distances – a shame, given that in other respects the Black makes a fine super-GT. More concerning still is that over the most extreme of our ride routes, the SL struggled to keep its driven wheels on the deck, causing the ESP to work overtime.

BUYING AND OWNING

★★★☆☆

Only eight are coming to the UK and all are sold. Depreciation is something of an unknown; the 'standard' SL65 is a bit of a shocker, losing more than 50 per cent of its value in the first year, but relative scarcity should help the Black. Running costs are unlikely to trouble those who can afford the purchase price, but a best of 22.1mpg and worst of 9.5mpg actually compares favourably with rivals. Service intervals remain every 15,000 miles.

Mercedes-Benz SL65

AUTOCAR VERDICT ★★★☆☆
Awe-inspiring and desirable, but oddly disappointing

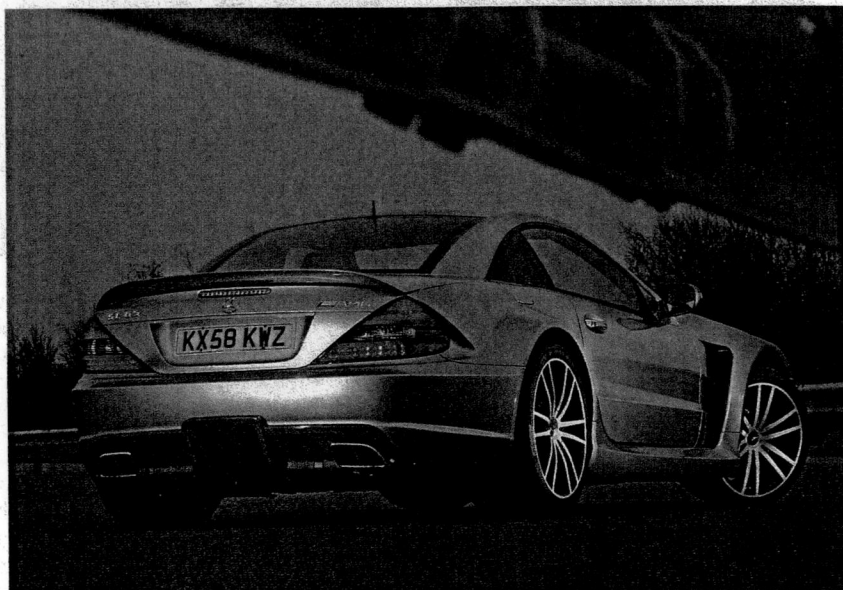

There can be no doubt that the SL65 Black Series is an extremely thrilling, charming car. Its styling may be a little over the top – cartoonish, even – but you cannot question the attention to detail or the extent to which Mercedes' AMG division has gone to make the ultimate SL. The extensive use of carbonfibre and the dramatic weight loss go some way to justifying the cost, more so than the upgrades to the engine.

What is more difficult to pin down is exactly what, beyond its flagship status, the SL65 Black is meant to represent. Mercedes says the car will spend more time on track than off, but from our experience it isn't quite the track tool we'd hoped it might be; there isn't quite the involvement you'd expect. All of which wouldn't be such an issue if the SL65 cut it as a road car, but in the spec we tried, at least, an overly firm ride rules this out.

TESTERS' NOTES

JAMIE CORSTORPH
Sitting in what for the part looks like an ord SL cabin, it's easy to f the extra width – un look in the wing mirr

MATT PRIOR
Curiously, Mercedes repositioned the star button from the top c the gear selector.

VICKY PARROTT
Equipment is import but AMG could have yet more weight by f fixed spoiler and rem the electric motors.

JOBS FOR THE FAC

● Fit a transmissi that allows more throttle control.
● Offer switchable dampers for road
● Sort out the lar turning circle.

AUTOCAR ROAD TEST TOP FIVE

MAKE	1st FERRARI	2nd LAMBORGHINI	3rd PAGANI	4th KOENIGSEGG	5th MERCEDES-BENZ
Model	599 GTB	Murciélago LP640	ZONDA F	CCX	SL65 AMG Black Se
Price	£193,234	£197,460	£390,000	£415,000	£249,500
Power	611bhp at 7600rpm	631bhp at 8000rpm	593bhp at 6150rpm	806bhp at 7000rpm	661bhp at 5400rpm
Torque	448lb ft at 5600rpm	437lb ft at 6000rpm	561lb ft at 4000rpm	693lb ft at 5500rpm	737lb ft at 2200-420
0-60mph	3.7sec	3.5sec	3.6sec (claimed to 62mph)	3.2sec (claimed to 62mph)	4.2sec
Top speed	205mph+ (claimed)	210mph (claimed)	214mph (claimed)	245mph+ (claimed)	200mph (claimed)
Fuel consumption	11.8mpg (combined)	12.3mpg (combined)	na	16mpg (combined)	19.6mpg (combined)
Kerb weight	1690kg (claimed)	1765kg (claimed)	1230kg (claimed)	1280kg (claimed)	1870kg (claimed)
CO$_2$/tax band	490g/km, 35 per cent	495g/km, 35 per cent	na	na	344g/km, 35 per cer
	Ferrari's finest is the most captivating front-engined road car on sale. ★★★★★	Amazing pace, accessible handling and old-school supercar looks. ★★★★☆	Beautifully engineered, great engine, fine handling, but pricey. ★★★★☆	Expensive, but pace and rarity value almost justify it. ★★★★☆	Great sense of dram satisfies neither tr nor GT requiremen ★★★☆

Every Top Five See Page 78